The Creation of Sacred Literature

Composition and Redaction of the Biblical Text

The Creation of
Sacred Literature

Composition and Redaction
of the Biblical Text

Edited by Richard Elliott Friedman

UNIVERSITY OF CALIFORNIA PRESS

Berkeley · Los Angeles · London

UNIVERSITY OF CALIFORNIA PUBLICATIONS: NEAR EASTERN STUDIES

Volume 22

UNIVERSITY OF CALIFORNIA PRESS
BERKELEY AND LOS ANGELES
CALIFORNIA

UNIVERSITY OF CALIFORNIA PRESS, LTD.
LONDON ENGLAND

ISBN 0-520-09637-1
LIBRARY OF CONGRESS CATALOG CARD NUMBER: 81-2547

© 1981 BY THE REGENTS OF THE UNIVERSITY OF CALIFORNIA
PRINTED IN THE UNITED STATES OF AMERICA

Library of Congress Cataloging in Publication Data

The Creation of sacred literature.

(University of California publications, Near
Eastern studies; v. 22)
  Includes bibliographical references.
  1. Bible. O.T.—Criticism, interpretation, etc.—
Addresses. essays, lectures. I. Friedman, Richard E.
II. Series.
BS1192.C73   221.6   81-2547
ISBN 0-520-09637-1   AACR2

Contents

CONCLUSION

Introduction:
Sacred History/Sacred Literature

RICHARD ELLIOTT FRIEDMAN

Besides everything else that the Hebrew Bible is, it has probably the most extraordinary literary history of any book. Whatever view one holds with regard to the background of the sources of the biblical narrative books, there is hardly a biblical scholar left in the world who does not at least see in some or all of these books a rich composite of layers. The joining of various traditions, of prose and poetry, history and fiction, into a continuous account of the relations of the God Yhwh with the human community is an accomplishment to be admired no less than the composition of the component stories themselves. Biblical narrative is the product of a literary partnership of author and arranger (editor, redactor). Each makes a critical contribution to the creation of the book. The more we learn of the art of the redactors, identifying the techniques of arrangement, inclusion, narrative resumption, framing-documents, and others, the more we appreciate the skill with which these individuals created the Bible out of the traditions they inherited.

The study of the Bible is thus at a vital juncture. On the one hand, it is not the sources J or P that we read in the final analysis, but the Torah. Exegesis is ultimately of the Bible, not of its sources. On the other hand, it is difficult to read the text of the Bible ignoring all along what we know of its own story. Nor is this knowledge any longer limited to scholars. Especially in the present generation, numbers of students are introduced to historical and literary-critical study of the Bible. Critical editions of the biblical text and critical commentaries are widely available. It is becoming necessary to read the book on both levels simultaneously. It is precisely at this juncture that study which focuses upon redaction, i.e., upon the manner of formulation of received texts into a coherent, meaningful whole, can be of value.

One confronts questions of conception. What did the author of any given portion of the book perceive his work to be? Did he see himself as an historian, a narrator, an artist; in the service of history, God, the king, the people of Israel? One must then apply the same questions to the redactors. And in the final arrangement, do the authors' various contributions stand in harmony with one another or in tension? Are the conceptions of author and author, or author and redactor, at odds?

One confronts matters of technique as well. By what means did the redactor bring the received traditions together? To what extent did he inject his own interests into the text? Is the work which he created more—artistically, theologically—than the sum of its components?

Finally, one confronts questions of audience: two millennia of readers who have read the redactors' final literary product, critical readers of the last century. Is the book to be read as history, as literature? And as whose creation is it to be regarded: the authors', the redactors'?

These are the questions the seven writers of this volume address. At bottom, the question all of us are addressing is: in what way(s) is the study of the Bible different from the study of other literature? Courses are offered under the title "The Bible as Literature," but we never have to offer a course titled "*War and Peace* as Literature." Presumably the difference is that most readers have perceived the Bible to be something else. If we identify this something else as *history*, we mislead. To the historian, it has been not a work of history but a source to be used in writing history. To the pious, it has been more than history; it is sacred. Indeed, it is a strange history which resides between the same covers as the Psalms, Proverbs, and Ecclesiastes, as well as including poetry, such as the Blessing of Jacob, the Song of Moses, and the Song of Deborah, and legislation, such as that of Leviticus, distributed through the narrative itself. A book whose every sentence of prose and line of poetry is assigned a chapter-and-verse number for careful reference is perceived to be more than history or literature, though it contain both.

In part, the difference in calling this book *sacred* is in the perception of origin, i.e., the relationship between the text and its authors. The book is held to be divinely revealed or inspired, or even of human origin but nonetheless composed in devotion to divinity. In part, the difference lies in the perception of authority, i.e., the relationship between the text and its readers. The text is prescriptive. The characters are models; the stories are didactic or edifying; the codes are normative. It is not just another book among books, not "a great book." One cannot impress a pious Christian or orthodox Jew by praising it as "one of the greatest books in the world." To the pious, the Bible is not to be measured in the category of other books, because, by virtue of origin and authority, it transcends other books.

The discussion of this regard for the book as sacred is not limited to the perceptions of reverent readers. The writers (or at least some of them) and, perhaps more important, the editors who finally constructed the work joined knowingly in a prescriptive, authoritative enterprise. We run little risk of the intentional fallacy in speaking of a book which includes the declaration "Thou shalt not steal" as having been meant to be normative. The combination of legislation with narrative itself affirms that the authors and editors sought more than historical annals. Their formulation of the biblical covenants in the structure of ancient Near Eastern international treaty documents, i.e., in the dominant mode of legal discourse of the time,[1] further points to their sense of the authoritative quality of their product.

Indeed, the perceptions of the secular reader figure in the matter of the regard for the book as sacred as well. Insofar as the book is "charged" in the eyes of so many among its readers—and was so designed by its authors and redactors—the secular reader hardly reads the book in a vacuum. One comes to the book in embrace of the tradition or in response to it in almost every case. This is not to say that one cannot read the Bible with objectivity but only that one reads it with consciousness of its singular character.

---

1. See G. E. Mendenhall, *Law and Covenant in Israel and the Ancient Near East* (Pittsburgh, 1955), and Klaus Baltzer, *The Covenant Formulary* (Philadelphia, 1971).

Thus, the considerations that figure centrally in our discussion in this volume are, first, that biblical narrative has the character of both literature and history; second, that its authorship is composite and singularly complex editorially; and third, that its creators and the majority of its readers have held it as sacred.

The first three essays are broad, synthetic studies of the composition of individual biblical stories and the redaction of the larger complexes of narrative. These are followed by three case studies. The concluding essay treats the impact of understanding the Bible's literary history on the reading of the final product.

SYNTHETIC STUDIES

Sacred History and Prose Fiction*

ROBERT ALTER

The Hebrew Bible is generally perceived, with considerable justice, as sacred history, and both terms of that status have often been invoked to argue against the applicability to the Bible of the methods of literary analysis. If the text is sacred, if it was grasped by the audiences for whom it was made as a revelation of God's will, perhaps of His literal words, how can one hope to explain it through categories developed for the understanding of such a fundamentally secular, individual, and aesthetic enterprise as modern Western literature? And if the text is history, seriously purporting to render an account of the origins of things and of Israelite national experience as they actually happened, is it not presumptuous to analyze these narratives in the terms we customarily apply to prose fiction, a mode of writing we understand to be the arbitrary invention of the writer, whatever the correspondences it may exhibit with quotidian or even historical reality? In a novel by Flaubert or Tolstoy or Henry James, where we are aware of the conscious fashioning of a fictional artifice, sometimes with abundant documentation from the writer's notebooks and letters, it is altogether appropriate to discuss techniques of characterization, shifts in narrative point of view, the artful manipulation of dialogue, the ordering of larger compositional elements, but are we not coercing the Bible into being "literature" by attempting to transfer such categories to a set of texts that are theologically motivated, historically oriented, and perhaps to some extent collectively composed?

At least some of these objections will be undercut by recognizing, as several recent analysts have argued, that history is far more intimately related to fiction than we have been accustomed to assume. It is important to see the common ground shared by the two modes of narrative, ontologically and formally, but it also strikes me as misguided to insist that writing history is finally identical with writing fiction. The two kinds of literary activity obviously share a whole range of narrative strategies, and the historian may seem to resemble the writer of fiction in employing, as in some ways he must, a series of imaginative constructs. Yet there remains a qualitative difference, for example, between G. M. Trevelyan's portrait of Robert Walpole, which, though an interpretation and so in some degree an imaginative projection, is closely bound to the known historical facts, and Fielding's Jonathan Wild, a character that alludes satirically to Walpole but clearly has its own dynamics as an independent fictional invention.

*© 1981 by Robert Alter. This text also appears, in a somewhat modified form, in Robert Alter's *The Art of Biblical Narrative*, published by Basic Books.

The case of the Bible's sacred history, however, is rather different from that of modern historiography. There is, to begin with, a whole spectrum of relations to history in the sundry biblical narratives, as I shall try to indicate later, but none of these involves the sense of being bound to documentable facts that characterizes history in its modern acceptation. It is often asserted that the biblical writer is bound instead to the fixed materials, whether oral or written, that tradition has transmitted to him. This is a claim difficult to verify or refute because we have no real way of knowing what were the precise contents of Hebrew tradition around the beginning of the first millennium B.C.E. A close inspection, however, of the texts that have been passed down to us may lead to a certain degree of skepticism about this scholarly notion of the tyrannical authority of ancient tradition, may lead us, in fact, to conclude that the writers exercised a good deal of artistic freedom in articulating the traditions at their disposal.

As odd as it may sound at first, I would contend that prose fiction is the best general rubric for describing biblical narrative. Or, to be more precise, and to borrow a key term from Herbert Schneidau's speculative, sometimes questionable, often suggestive study, *Sacred Discontent*, we can speak of the Bible as *historicized* prose fiction. To cite the clearest example, the Patriarchal narratives may be composite fictions based on national traditions, but in the writers' refusal to make them conform to the symmetries of expectation, in their contradictions and anomalies, they suggest the unfathomability of life in history under an inscrutable God. "What we are witnessing in Genesis, and in parts of the David story," Schneidau observes, "is the birth of a new kind of historicized fiction, moving steadily away from the motives and habits of the world of legend and myth."[1] This generalization can, I think, be extended beyond Genesis and the David story to most of biblical narrative, even where, as in parts of the Book of Kings, an abundance of legendary material is evident. Because the central thesis of Schneidau's book is the rebellion of biblical literature against the pagan world-view, which is locked into an eternal cyclical movement, his stress falls on the historicizing, though the fiction deserves equal attention. Indeed, as we shall have occasion to see, it may often be more precise to describe what happens in biblical narrative as fictionalized history, especially when we move into the period of the Judges and Kings. But before we pursue the theme of either history or fiction, we should pause over the prose component of prose fiction, which is far more than a matter of convenience in classification for the librarian.

It is peculiar, and culturally significant, that among ancient peoples only Israel should have chosen to cast its sacred national traditions in prose. Among many hazily conceived literary terms applied to the Bible, scholars have often spoken of it as the "national epic" of ancient Israel, or, more specifically, they have conjectured about an oral Creation epic and Exodus epic upon which the authors of the Pentateuch drew. But, as Shemaryahu Talmon has shrewdly argued, what by all appearances we have in the Bible is, quite to the contrary, a deliberate avoidance of epic, and the prose form of Hebrew narrative is the chief evidence for this avoidance:

> The ancient Hebrew writers purposefully nurtured and developed prose narration to take the place of the epic genre which by its content was intimately bound up with the world of paganism and appears to have had a special standing in the polytheistic cults. The recitation of the epics was tantamount to a reenactment of cosmic events in the manner of sympathetic

1. Baton Rouge, Louisiana, 1977, p. 215.

magic. In the process of total rejection of the polytheistic religions and their ritual expressions in the cult, epic songs and also the epic genre were purged from the repertoire of the Hebrew authors.[2]

What is crucial for the literary understanding of the Bible is that this reflex away from the polytheistic genre had powerfully constructive consequences in the new medium which the ancient Hebrew writers fashioned for their monotheistic purposes. Prose narration, affording writers a remarkable range and flexibility in the means of presentation, could be utilized to liberate fictional personages from the fixed choreography of timeless events and thus could transform storytelling from ritual rehearsal to the delineation of the wayward paths of human freedom, the quirks and contradictions of men and women seen as moral agents and complex centers of motive and feeling.

The underlying impulse of this whole portentous transition in literary modes is effectively caught, though with certain imprecisions I shall try to correct, by Schneidau in an anthropological generalization that nicely complements Talmon's historical proposal. Schneidau speaks of a "world of linked analogies and correspondences" manifested in the primitive imagination and in the divinatory mode of expression. "A cosmology of hierarchical continuities, as in mythological thought, exhibits strong metaphorical tendencies. The enmeshing and interlocking of structures is coherently expressed in poetic evocation of transferable, substitutable qualities and names. In this world, movement tends to round itself into totalization, impelled by the principle of closure." In contrast to this mythological world dominated by metaphor, Schneidau sees metonymy, with its point-to-point movement suggesting the prosaic modes of narrative and history, as the key to the literature of the Bible, a literature that breaks away from the old cosmic hierarchies. He attempts to summarize this contrast in an aphorism: "Where myth is hypotactic metaphors, the Bible is paratactic metonymies."[3] That is, where myth involves a set of equivalencies arranged in some system of subordination, the Bible offers a series of contiguous terms arranged in sequence without a clear definition of the link between one term and the next.

This general comparison provides an important insight into the innovative nature of the Bible's literary enterprise, but some of the terms invoked are a little misleading. There are, to begin with, a good many ancient Near Eastern narratives which are sophisticated, fundamentally secular literary works, though for Schneidau as for Talmon the mythological poems would appear to be the paradigm of pagan literature from which the Bible swerves. The paradigmatic function of this particular kind of pre-Israelite narrative may well justify the stress on the Hebrew literary rejection of myth, but other terms that Schneidau adopts remain problematic. Roman Jakobson's schematic distinction between metaphor and metonymy fits the case under discussion only in a loose figurative sense because actual metaphor (rather than inferable metaphysical "correspondences") is by no means predominant in the extant ancient Near Eastern mythological epics. Similarly, hypotaxis and parataxis may be logically coordinated with metaphor and metonymy, respectively, but in actual syntactic patterns the Near Eastern mythological verse narratives would appear to be mainly paratactic, while biblical narrative prose exhibits a good deal of variation from parataxis to

2. "The 'Comparative Method' in Biblical Interpretation—Principles and Problems," *Göttingen Congress Volume* (Leiden, 1978), p. 354.
3. Schneidau, *Sacred Discontent,* p. 292.

hypotaxis, according to the aims of the writer and the requirements of the particular narrative juncture. Schneidau's most valuable perception, in any case, is not dependent on these terms, for his main point is the vigorous movement of biblical writing away from the stable closure of the mythological world and toward the indeterminacy, the shifting causal concatenations, the ambiguities of a fiction made to resemble the uncertainties of life in history. And for that movement, I would add, the suppleness of prose as a narrative medium was indispensable, at least in the Near Eastern setting.

One final qualification should be added to this instructive if somewhat overdrawn opposition between myth and "historicized fiction." Different cultures often take different routes to what is substantially the same end; and if one moves beyond the ancient Fertile Crescent to the Greek sphere, one can find in sophisticated mythographic verse-narratives, such as Hesiod and the mythological episodes in Homer, a good deal in the treatment of motive, character, and causation that is analogous to the biblical sense of indeterminacy and ambiguity. The Hebrew writers, however, made a special virtue in this regard out of the newly fashioned prose medium in which they worked, and this deserves closer attention than it has generally received.

As an initial illustration of how the modalities of prose fiction operate in biblical narrative, I should like to consider a passage from the so-called primeval history, the creation of Eve (Genesis 2). It may serve as a useful test-case because with its account of origins, its generalized human figures, its anthropormorphic deity, and with the Mesopotamian background of the version of creation in which it occurs, it has been variously classified by modern commentators as myth, legend, and folklore, and would seem quite unlike what we usually think of as artfully conceived fiction. In the immediately preceding verse, one recalls, God had warned Adam under penalty of death not to eat from the Tree of Knowledge. Man's response to this injunction is not recorded. Instead, the narrative moves on—perhaps making that hiatus itself a proleptic intimation of the link between Adam's future mate and the seizing of forbidden knowledge—to an expression in direct speech of God's concern for the solitary condition of his creature:

> 18. The Lord God said, "It is not good for man to be alone. I shall make him an aid fit for him. 19. And the Lord God formed from the earth every beast of the field and every bird of the sky and He brought them to the man to see what he would call them; and whatever the man called a living creature would be its name. 20. The man called names to all the cattle and to the birds of the sky and to every beast of the field, but for the man no fit aid was found. 21. And the Lord God cast a deep slumber upon the man and he slept; and He took one of his ribs and closed up the flesh at that place. 22. And the Lord God fashioned the rib he had taken from the man into a woman and He brought her to the man. 23. The man said:

> > This one at last
> > bone of my bones
> > and flesh of my flesh.
> > This one shall be called woman
> > for from man was this one taken.

> 24. Thus does a man leave his father and mother and cling to his woman, and they become one flesh. 25. And the two of them were naked, the man and his woman, and they were not ashamed.

The usual taxonomic approach to the Bible would explain the whole passage as a piece of ancient folklore, an etiological tale intended to account for the existence of woman, for her subordinate status, and for the attraction she perennially exerts over man. The inset of formal verse (a common convention in biblical narrative for direct speech that has some significantly summarizing or ceremonial function) in fact looks archaic, and could conceivably have been a familiar etiological tag in circulation for centuries before the making of this passage. Folkloric traditions may very well be behind the text, but I do not think that in themselves they provide a very satisfactory sense of the artful complex that the writer has shaped out of his materials. Our first ancestors of course cannot be allowed much individuality and so they are not exactly "fictional characters" in the way that later figures in Genesis like Jacob and Joseph and Tamar will be. Nevertheless, the writer, through a subtle manipulation of language and narrative exposition, manages to endow Adam and Eve with a degree of morally problematic interiority one would hardly expect in a primitive folktale explaining origins. Before we look at some of the details, we might contrast the general impression of this passage with the account of the creation of mankind (there is no separate creation of woman) in the *Enuma Elish*, the Babylonian creation epic. The god Marduk, after triumphing over the primeval mother Tiamat, announces:

> Blood I will mass and cause bones to be.
> I will establish a savage, "man" shall be his name.
> Verily, savage-man I will create.
> He shall be charged with the service of the gods
>   That they might be at ease.[4]

Marduk shares with the God of Israel the anthropomorphic métier of a sculptor in the medium of flesh and bone, but man in the Akkadian verse narrative is merely an object acted upon, his sole reason for existence to supply the material wants of the gods. Humanity is conceived here exclusively in terms of ritual function—man is made in order to offer sacrifices to the gods—and so the highly differentiated realms of history and moral action are not intimated in the account of man's creation. This is a signal instance of what Schneidau means by humanity's being locked into a set of fixed hierarchies in the mythological world-view. Man so conceived cannot be the protagonist of prose fiction: the appropriate narrative medium is mythological epic, in which the stately progression of parallelistic verse—in fact, predominantly paratactic and unmetaphorical here—emphatically rehearses man's eternal place in an absolute cosmic scheme. (Of course, few mythological epics will correspond so neatly to these notions of fixity and closure. But the model of the *Enuma Elish* is decisive for our text because it reflects the prevalent norm of sacred narrative with which the Hebrew writer was breaking.) If we now return to Genesis 2, we can clearly see how the monotheistic writer works not only with very different theological assumptions but also with a radically different sense of literary form.

In contrast to the hortatory diction of Marduk and his fellow-members of the Babylonian pantheon, God expresses His perception of man's condition and His own intention with a stark directness: "It is not good for man to be alone. I shall make him an aid

---

4. Translation by E. A. Speiser, *Ancient Near Eastern Texts Relating to the Old Testament*, ed. J. B. Pritchard (Princeton, 1950), p. 66.

fit for him." (His utterance, nevertheless, is close enough to a scannable verse of complementary parallelism to give it a hint of formal elevation.) Then there occurs a peculiar interruption. We have been conditioned by the previous version of cosmogony to expect an immediate act of creation to flow from the divine utterance that is introduced by the formula, "And God said." Here, however, we must wait two verses for the promised creation of a helpmate while we follow the process of man giving names to all living creatures. These verses (19 and 20) are marked, as a formal seal of their integration in the story, by an envelope structure, being immediately preceded by the thematically crucial phrase ʿēzer kᵊnegdô (literally, "an aid alongside him") and concluding with that same phrase. A concise comment on these two verses in the classical Midrash nicely reflects their strategic utility: "He made them pass by in pairs. He said, 'Everything has its partner but I have no partner'" (*Bereshit Rabba* 17:5). What is especially interesting about this miniature dramatization in the Midrash is where it might have come from in the text. For the literary insights of the midrashic exegetes generally derive from their sensitive response to verbal clues—in the recurrence of a key word, the nuanced choice of a particular lexical item, significant sound-play, and so forth. Here, however, it seems that the Midrash is responding not to any particular word in the passage but to an aspect of the text continuum which today we would call a strategy of narrative exposition. Eve has been promised. She is then withheld for two carefully framed verses while God allows man to perform his unique function as the bestower of names on things. There is implicit irony in this order of narrated events. Man is superior to all other living creatures because only he can invent language, only he has the level of consciousness that makes him capable of linguistic ordering. But this very consciousness makes him aware of his solitude in contrast to the rest of the zoological kingdom. (It is, perhaps, a solitude mitigated but not entirely removed by the creation of woman, for that creation takes place through the infliction of a kind of wound on him, and afterward, in historical time, he will pursue her, strain to become "one flesh" with her, as though to regain a lost part of himself.) The contrast between mateless man calling names to a mute world of mated creatures is brought out by a finesse of syntax not reproducible in translation. Verse 20 actually tells us that man gave names "to all cattle . . . to birds . . . to beast . . . to the man," momentarily seeming to place Adam in an anaphoric prepositional series with all living creatures. This incipient construal is then reversed by the verb "did not find," which sets man in opposition to all that has preceded. One could plausibly argue, then, that the Midrash was not merely indulging in a flight of fancy when it imagined Adam making that confession of loneliness as he named the creatures passing before him.

When God at last begins to carry out His promise, at the beginning of verse 21, man, with the intervention of divine anaesthetic, is reduced from a conscious agent to an inert object acted upon, for the moment much like man in the *Enuma Elish*. The thematic difference, of course, is that this image of man as passive matter is bracketed on both sides by his performances as master of language. As soon as the awakened man discovers woman, he proceeds—as natural births elsewhere in the Bible are regularly followed by the ceremony of naming—to name her, adopting the formal emphasis of a poem. The poem, whether or not it was the writer's original composition, fits beautifully into the thematic argument of his narrative. Written in a double chiastic structure, it refers to the woman just being named by an indicative, ōʾt, "this [feminine] one," which is the first and last word of the poem in the Hebrew as well as the linchpin in the middle. Man names the animals over whom he has dominion; he names woman, over whom he ostensibly will have dominion. But in the poem, man and his bone and flesh are syntactically surrounded by this new female presence, a rhetorical configuration that makes perfect sense in the light of their subsequent history together.

The explanatory verse 24, which begins with "thus" (*ʿal kēn*), a fixed formula for introducing etiological assertions, might well have been part of a proverbial statement adopted verbatim by the writer, but even if this hypothesis is granted, what is remarkable is the artistry with which he weaves the etiological utterance into the texture of his own prose. The splendid image of desire fulfilled and, by extension, of the conjugal state—"they become one flesh"—is both a vivid glimpse of the act itself and a bold hyperbole. The writer, I would suggest, is as aware of the hyperbolic aspect of the image as later Plato will be when in *The Symposium* he attributes to Aristophanes the notion that lovers are the bifurcated halves of a primal self who are trying to recapture that impossible primal unity. For as soon as the idea of one flesh has been put forth (and "one" is the last word of the verse in the Hebrew), the narration proceeds as follows: "And the two of them were naked, the man and his woman, and they were not ashamed." After being invoked as the timeless model of conjugal oneness, they are immediately seen as two, a condition stressed by the deliberately awkward and uncharacteristic doubling back of the syntax in the appositional phrase, "the man and his woman"—a small illustration of how the flexibility of the prose medium enables the writer to introduce psychological distinctions, dialectical reversals of thematic direction, that would not have been feasible in the verse narratives of the ancient Near East. So the first man and woman are now two, vulnerable in their two-ness to the temptation of the serpent, who will be able to seduce first one, and through the one, the other: naked (*ʿărûmmîm*), unashamed, they are about to be exposed to the most cunning (*ʿārûm*) of the beasts of the field, who will give them cause to feel shame.

From this distance in time, it is impossible to determine how much of this whole tale was sanctified, even verbally fixed, tradition; how much was popular lore perhaps available in different versions; how much the original invention of the writer. What a close reading of the text does suggest, however, is that the writer could manipulate his inherited materials with sufficient freedom and sufficient firmness of authorial purpose to define motives, relations, and unfolding themes, even in a primeval history, with the kind of subtle cogency we associate with the conscious artistry of the narrative mode designated prose fiction. (Here and in what follows, I assume when I say "conscious artistry" that there is always a complex interplay between deliberate intention and unconscious intuition in the act of artistic creation; but the biblical writer is no different from his modern counterpart in this regard.) Throughout these early chapters of Genesis, Adam and Eve are not the fixed figures of legend or myth but are made to assume contours conceived in the writer's particularizing imagination through the brief but revealing dialogue he invents for them and through the varying strategies of presentation he adopts in reporting their immemorial acts.

Let me hasten to say that in giving such weight to fictionality, I do not mean to discount the historical impulse that informs the Hebrew Bible. The God of Israel, as so often has been observed, is above all the God of history: the working out of His purposes in history is a process that compels the attention of the Hebrew imagination, which is thus led to the most vital interest in the concrete and differential character of historical events. The point is that fiction was the principal means the biblical authors had at their disposal for realizing history.[5] Under scrutiny, biblical narrative generally proves to be either fiction laying claim to a place in the chain of causation and the realm of moral consequentiality that belong to history, as in the primeval history—the tales of the Patriarchs and much of the Exodus story and the account of the early Conquest—or history being given the imaginative definition of fiction, as in most of the narratives from the period of the Judges onward. This schema, of course, is necessarily neater than the persistently untidy reality of the variegated biblical narratives. What the Bible offers us is an uneven continuum and a constant interweave of factual historical detail (especially, but by no means exclusively, for the later periods) with purely legendary "history"; occasional enigmatic vestiges of mythological lore; etiological stories; archetypal fictions of the founding fathers of the nation; folktales of heroes and wonder-working men of God; verisimilar inventions of wholly fictional personages attached to the progress of national history; and fictionalized versions of known historical figures. All of these narratives are presented as history, that is, as things that really happened and that have some significant consequence for human or Israelite destiny. The only evident exceptions to this rule are Job, which in its very stylization seems manifestly a philosophic fable (hence the rabbinic dictum, "There was no such creature as Job; he is a parable"), and Jonah, which with its satiric and fantastic exaggerations looks like a parabolic illustration of the prophetic calling and of God's universality.

Despite the variegated character of these narratives, composed as they were by many different hands over a period of several centuries, I would like to attempt a rough generalization about the kind of literary project they constitute. The ancient Hebrew writers, as I have already intimated, seek through the process of narrative realization to reveal the enactment of God's purposes in historical events. This enactment, however, is continuously complicated by a perception of two, approximately parallel, dialectical tensions. One is a tension between the divine plan and the disorderly character of actual historical events, or, to translate this opposition into specifically biblical terms, between the divine promise and its ostensible failure to be fulfilled; the other is a tension between God's will, His providential guidance, and human freedom, the refractory nature of man.

If one may presume at all to reduce great achievements to a common denominator, it might be possible to say that the depth with which human nature is imagined in the Bible is a function of its being conceived caught in the powerful interplay of this double dialectic between design and disorder, providence and freedom. The various biblical narratives in fact may be usefully seen as forming a spectrum between the opposing extremes of disorder and design. Toward the disorderly end of things, where the recalcitrant facts of known history have to be encompassed, including specific political movements, military triumphs and reversals, and the like, would be Judges, Samuel, and Kings. In these books, the narrators and on occasion some of the personages struggle quite explicitly to reconcile their knowledge of the divine promise with their

---

5. A recent book by Jacob Licht, *Storytelling in the Bible* (Jerusalem, 1978), proposes that the "historical aspect" and the "storytelling" or "aesthetic" aspect of biblical narrative be thought of as entirely discrete functions that can be neatly peeled apart for inspection—one gathers, like the different colored strands of electrical wiring. This facile separation of the inseparable suggests how little some Bible scholars have thought about the role of literary art in biblical literature.

awareness of what is actually happening in history. At the other end of the spectrum, near the pole of design, one might place the Book of Esther. This post-Exilic story, which presents itself as a piece of political history affecting the main diaspora community, is in fact a kind of fairytale—the lovely damsel, guided by a wise godfather, who is made queen and saves her people—richly embellished with satiric invention; its comic art departs from historical verisimilitude in ways that pre-Exilic Hebrew narrative seldom does, and the story demonstrates God's providential power in history with a schematic neatness unlike that of earlier historicized fiction in the Bible.

Somewhere toward the middle of this spectrum would be Genesis, where the sketchiness of the known historical materials allows considerable latitude for the elucidation of a divine plan in them, with, however, this sense of design repeatedly counterbalanced by the awareness of man's unruly nature, the perilous and imperious individuality of the various human agents in the divine experiment. Individuality is played against providential design in a rather different fashion in the Book of Ruth. Ruth, Naomi, and Boaz are fictional inventions, probably based on no more than names, if that, preserved in national memory. In the brief span of this narrative, they exhibit in speech and action traits of character that make them memorable individuals, as the more schematically conceived Esther and Mordecai are not. But in their plausible individuality they also become exemplary figures, thus earning themselves a place in the national history: Ruth through her steadfastness and Boaz through his kindness and his adherence to the procedures of legitimate succession make themselves the justified progenitors of the line of David. The Book of Ruth, then, which we might place near Genesis toward the pole of design in our imaginary spectrum, is, because of its realistic psychology and its treatment of actual social institutions, a verisimilar historicized fiction, while the Book of Esther seems more a comic fantasy utilizing pseudo-historical materials.

Let me risk a large conjecture, if only because it may help us get a clearer sighting on the phenomenon we are considering. It may be that a sense of some adequate dialectical tension between these antitheses of divine plan and the sundry disorders of human performance in history served as an implicit criterion for deciding which narratives were to be regarded as canonical. It would be an understatement to say we possess only scanty information about the now lost body of uncanonical ancient Hebrew literature, but the few hints the Bible itself provides would seem to point in two opposite directions. On the one hand, in Kings we are repeatedly told that details skimped in the narrative at hand can be discovered by referring to the Chronicles of the Kings of Judah and the Chronicles of the Kings of Israel. Those books, one may assume, were excluded from the authoritative national tradition and hence not preserved because they were court histories, probably partisan in character, and erred on the side of the cataloguing of historical events without an informing vision of God's design working through history. On the other hand, brief and enigmatic allusion with citation is made in Numbers, Joshua, and Samuel to the Book of Yashar and the Book of the Battles of Yhwh. The latter sounds as though it was a list of military triumphs with God as principal actor; the former, to judge by the two fragments quoted (Josh 10:13; 2 Sam 1:18), was probably a verse narrative, perhaps a martial epic with miraculous elements. I would venture to guess that both books were felt to be too legendary, too committed to the direct narrative tracing of God's design, without a sufficient counterweight of the mixed stuff of recognizable historical experience.

Let us direct our attention now to the Bible's historical narratives proper in order to understand more concretely what is implied by the fictional component in describing them as historicized fiction. The large cycle of stories about David, which is surely one of the most stunning imaginative achievements of ancient literature, provides an instructive central instance of the intertwining of history and fiction. This narrative, though it may have certain folkloric embellishments (such as David's victory over Goliath) is based on firm historical facts, as modern research has tended to confirm: there really was a David who fought a civil war against the house of Saul, achieved undisputed sovereignty over the twelve tribes, conquered Jerusalem, founded a dynasty, created a small empire, and was succeeded by his son Solomon. Beyond these broad outlines, it is quite possible that many of the narrated details about David, including matters bearing on the complications of his conjugal life and his relations with his children, may have been reported on good authority.

Nevertheless, these stories are not, strictly speaking, historiography but rather the imaginative reenactment of history by a gifted writer who organizes his materials along certain thematic biases and according to his own remarkable intuition of the psychology of the characters. He feels entirely free, one should remember, to invent interior monologue for his characters; to ascribe feeling, intention, or motive to them when he chooses; to supply verbatim dialogue (and he is one of literature's masters of dialogue) for occasions when no one but the actors themselves could have had knowledge of exactly what was said. The author of the David stories stands in basically the same relation to Israelite history as Shakespeare stands to English history in his history plays. Shakespeare was obviously not free to have Henry V lose the battle of Agincourt or to allow someone else to lead the English forces there, but, working from the hints of historical tradition, he could invent a kind of *Bildungsroman* for the young Prince Hal; surround him with invented characters who would serve as foils, mirrors, obstacles, aids in his development; create a language and a psychology for the king which are the writer's own achievement, making out of the stuff of history a powerful projection of human possibility. That is essentially what the author of the David cycle does for David, Saul, Abner, Joab, Jonathan, Absalom, Michal, Abigail, and a host of other characters.

One memorable illustration among many of this transmutation of history into fiction is David's great confrontation with Saul at the cave in the wilderness of Ein Gedi (1 Samuel 24). The manic king, one recalls, while in pursuit of the young David, has gone into a cave to relieve himself, where by chance David and his men have taken refuge. David sneaks up to Saul and cuts off a corner of his robe. Then he is smitten with compunction for having perpetrated this symbolic mutilation on the anointed king, and he sternly holds his men in check while the unwitting Saul walks off from the cave unharmed. Once the king is at a distance, David follows him out of the cave and, holding the excised corner of the robe, he hails Saul, and shouts out to his erstwhile pursuer one of his most remarkable speeches, in which he expresses fealty and reverence to the Lord's anointed one, disavows any evil intention toward him (with the corner of the robe as evidence of what he could have done and did not), and proclaims his own humble status: "After whom did the king of Israel set out?" he says in verse-like symmetry, "After whom are you chasing? After a dead dog, after a single flea?"

At the end of this relatively lengthy speech, the narrator holds us in suspense for still another moment by choosing to preface Saul's response with a chain of introductory phrases: "And it came to pass when David finished speaking these words that Saul said"—and then what he says has a breathtaking brevity after David's stream of words, and constitutes one of those astonishing reversals that make the rendering of character in these stories so arresting: " 'Is it your voice, David, my son?' and Saul raised his voice and wept." The point is not merely that the author has made up dialogue to which he could have had no "documentary" access: Thucydides, after all, does that as a stylized technique of representing the various positions maintained by different historical personages. In the biblical story the invented dialogue is an expression of the author's imaginative grasp of his protagonists as distinctive moral and psychological figures, of their emotion-fraught human intercourse dramatically conceived; and what that entire process of imagination essentially means is the creation of fictional character.

As elsewhere in biblical narrative, the revelation of character is effected with striking artistic economy, the specification of external circumstances, setting, and gesture held to a bare minimum, and dialogue made to carry a large part of the freight of meaning. To David's impassioned, elaborate rhetoric of self-justification, Saul responds with a kind of choked cry: "Is it your voice, David, my son?" Perhaps he asks this out of sheer amazement at what he has just heard, or because he is too far off to make out David's face clearly, or because his eyes are blinded with tears, which would be an apt emblem of the condition of moral blindness that has prevented him from seeing David as he really is. In connection with this last possibility, one suspects there is a deliberate if approximate echo of the blind Isaac's words to his son Jacob (after asking, "Who are you, my son?" Isaac proclaims, "The voice is the voice of Jacob"). The allusion, which complicates the meaning of the present encounter between an older and a younger man in a number of ways, is not one that an historical Saul would have been apt to make on the spot, but which a writer with the privilege of fictional invention could brilliantly contrive for this shadow-haunted king whose own firstborn son will not reign after him.

Perhaps it might be objected that the David stories are merely the exception that proves the rule—a sunburst of imaginative literary activity in a series of historical books which are, after all, chronicles of known events variously embroidered with folklore and underscored for theological emphasis. Let us consider then a passage from that long catalogue of military uprisings, the Book of Judges, where no serious claims could be made for complexity of characterization or for subtlety of thematic development, and see if we can still observe the modalities of prose fiction in what is told and how it is told. I should like to take the story of the assassination of Eglon King of Moab by Ehud the son of Gera (Judges 3). In the absence of convincing evidence to the contrary, let us assume the historical truth of the story, which seems plausible enough: that a tough, clever guerrilla leader named Ehud from the tribe of Benjamin, known for its martial skills, cut down Eglon more or less in the manner described, then mustered Israelite forces in the hill country of Ephraim for a successful rebellion, which was followed by a long period of relief from Moabite domination. Only the formulaic number of twice forty at the end ("And the land was quiet eighty years") would patently appear not to correspond to historical fact. Where, then, in this succinct political chronicle, is there room to talk about prose fiction? Here is how the main part of the story reads:

15. The Israelites cried out to the Lord, and He raised up a champion for them, Ehud the son of Gera the Benjaminite, a left-handed man. Now the Israelites sent tribute through him to Eglon King of Moab. 16. Ehud made himself a double-edged dagger a *gomed* long and strapped it under his garments on his right thigh. 17. He brought the tribute to Eglon King of Moab—and this Eglon was a very stout man. 18. And it came about that after he had finished presenting the tribute, he dismissed the people who had carried it. 19. And he had come from Pesilim near Gilgal. Then he said, "A secret word I have for you, King." "Silence!" he replied, and all his attendants went out. 20. Ehud came to him as he was sitting in his cool upper chamber all alone, and Ehud said, "A word of God I have for you," and he rose from his seat. 21. And Ehud reached with his left hand and took the dagger from his right thigh and thrust it into Eglon's belly. 22. The hilt went in after the blade and the fat closed over the blade, for he did not withdraw the dagger from the belly and the filth[6] burst out. 23. Ehud came out through the vestibule, closing the doors of the upper chamber on him and locking them. 24. He had just gone out when the courtiers came and saw that the doors were locked. "He is just relieving himself in the cool chamber," they said. 25. They waited a long time, and still he did not open the doors of the chamber. So they took the key and opened them, and, look, their lord was sprawled on the floor, dead.

It will be observed at once that the detailed attention given here to the implement and technique of killing, which would be normal in the *Iliad*, is rather uncharacteristic of the Hebrew Bible. One may assume that Ehud's bold resourcefulness in carrying out this assassination, which threw the Moabites into disarray and enabled the insurrection to succeed, was remarkable enough for the Chronicler to want to report it circumstantially. Each of the details, then, contributes to a clear understanding of just how the thing was done—clearer, of course, for the ancient audience than for us because we no longer have a coherent picture of the floor plan of the sort of Canaanite summer residence favored by Moabite kings and so we may have a little difficulty in reconstructing Ehud's entrances and exits. The left-handed Benjaminite warriors were known for their prowess, but Ehud also counts on his left-handedness as part of his strategy of surprise: a sudden movement of the left hand will not instantaneously be construed by the king as a movement of a weapon hand. Ehud also counts on the likelihood that Eglon will be inclined to trust him as a vassal bringing tribute and that the "secret" he promises to confide to the king will thus be understood as a piece of intelligence volunteered by an Israelite collaborator. The dagger or short sword (*ḥereb*) is of course strapped to Ehud's right thigh for easy drawing with the left hand; it is short enough to hide under his clothing, long enough to do Eglon's business without the killer's having to be unduly close to his victim, and double-edged to assure the lethality of one quick thrust. Eglon's encumbrance of fat will make him an easier target as he awkwardly rises from his seat, and perhaps Ehud leaves the weapon buried in the flesh in order not to splatter blood on himself, so that he can walk out through the vestibule unsuspected and make his escape. One commentator has ingeniously proposed that even the sordid detail of the release of the anal sphincter in the death spasm has its role in the exposition of the mechanics of the assassination: the courtiers outside, detecting the odor, assume that Eglon has locked the door because he is performing a bodily function, and so they wait long enough to enable Ehud to get away safely.[7]

6. There is a textual ambiguity here in the Hebrew.
7. Yehezkel Kaufmann, *The Book of Judges* (Hebrew) (Jerusalem, 1968), p. 109.

Yet if all this is the scrupulous report of an historical act of political terrorism, the writer has vividly thematized his historical material through a skillful manipulation of the prose-narrative medium. What emerges is not simply a circumstantial account of the Moabite king's destruction but a satiric vision of it at once shrewd and jubilant. The writer's imagination of the event is informed by an implicit etymologizing of Eglon's name, which suggests the Hebrew *ꜥēgel*, calf. The ruler of the occupying Moabite power turns out to be a fatted calf readied for slaughter—and perhaps even the epithet "stout," *bārîʾ*, is a play on *mᵊrîʾ*, "fatling," a sacrificial animal occasionally bracketed with calf. Eglon's fat is both the token of his physical ponderousness, his vulnerability to Ehud's sudden blade, and the emblem of his regal stupidity. Perhaps it may also hint at a kind of grotesque feminization of the Moabite leader: Ehud "comes to" the king, an idiom also used for sexual entry, and there is something hideously sexual about the description of the dagger-thrust. There may also be a deliberate sexual nuance in the "secret thing" Ehud brings to Eglon, in the way the two are locked together alone in a chamber, and in the sudden opening of locked entries at the conclusion of the story.[8]

Ehud's claim to have a secret message for the king is accepted immediately and without qualification by Eglon's confidential "Silence!" (or perhaps one might translate the onomatopoeic term as *sssh!*), the Moabite either failing to notice that Ehud has brusquely addressed him as "King" without the polite "My lord" (*ʾădōnî*) or construing this omission simply as evidence of Ehud's urgency. When the two are alone and Ehud again turns to Eglon, he drops even the bare title, flatly stating, "A word of God I have for you." This statement is a rather obvious but nevertheless effective piece of dramatic irony: the secret thing—the Hebrew term can mean word, message, thing—hidden beneath Ehud's garment is in fact the word of God that the divinely "raised" Benjaminite champion is about to bring home implacably to the corpulent king. Hearing that the promised political secret is actually an oracle, Eglon rises, perhaps in sheer eagerness to know the revelation, perhaps as an act of accepted decorum for receiving an oracular communication, and now Ehud can cut him down.

The courtiers' erroneous assumption that their bulky monarch is taking his leisurely time over the chamber pot is a touch of scatological humor at the expense of both king and followers, while it implicates them in the satiric portrayal of his credulity. This last effect is heightened by the presentation of their direct speech at the end of verse 24, and the switch of the narrative to their point of view in verses 23 and 24. Let me retranslate these clauses literally to reproduce the immediate effect of seeing the scene through their eyes that one experiences in the Hebrew: "The courtiers came and saw, look, the doors of the upper chamber are locked. . . . They waited a long time and, look, he's not opening the doors of the upper chamber, and they took the keys and opened them, and, look, their lord is sprawled on the floor, dead." The syntax of the concluding clause nicely follows the rapid stages of their perception as at last they are disabused of their illusion: first they see their king prostrate, and then they realize, climactically, that he is dead. An enemy's obtuseness is always an inviting target for satire in time of war, but here the exposure of Moabite stupidity has a double thematic function: to show the blundering helplessness of the pagan oppressor when faced with a liberator raised up by

8. The possible significance of locking and unlocking in the story was brought to my attention by George Savran.

the all-knowing God of Israel, and to demonstrate how these gullible Moabites, deprived of a leader, are bound to be inept in the war that immediately ensues.

In fact, great numbers of the Moabites are slaughtered at the fords of the Jordan, the location of the debacle perhaps suggesting that they allowed themselves to be drawn into an actual ambush, or, at any rate, that they foolishly rushed into places where the entrenched Israelites could hold them at a terrific strategic disadvantage. Ehud's assassination of Eglon, then, is not only connected causally with the subsequent Moabite defeat but it is also a kind of emblematic prefiguration of it. The link between the regicide and the war of liberation is reinforced by two punning verbal clues. Ehud thrusts (tq^c) the dagger into Eglon's belly, and as soon as he makes good his escape (verse 27), he blasts—the same verb, tq^c—the ram's horn to rally his troops.[9] The Israelites kill 10,000 Moabites, "everyone a lusty man and a brave man" (verse 29), but the word for "lusty," *šāmēn*, also means "fat," so the Moabites are "laid low [or subjugated] under the hand of Israel" (verse 30) in a neat parallel to the fate of their fat master under the swift left hand of Ehud. In all this, as I have said, it is quite possible that the writer faithfully represents the historical data without addition or substantive embellishment. The organization of the narrative, however, its lexical and syntactic choices, its small shifts in point of view, its brief but strategic uses of dialogue, produce an imaginative reenactment of the historical event, conferring upon it a strong attitudinal definition and discovering in it a pattern of meaning. It is perhaps less historicized fiction than fictionalized history—history in which the feeling and the meaning of events are concretely realized through the technical resources of prose fiction.

To round out this overview of the spectrum of fictional modalities in the Bible's sacred history, I should like to return to Genesis for a concluding illustration—this time, from the Patriarchal narratives, which, unlike the stories of the first ancestors of mankind, are firmly linked to Israelite national history. The linkage, to be sure, would appear to be more the writer's attribution than the result of any dependable historical traditions. Many modern scholars have assumed that the Patriarchs are the invented figures of early Hebrew folklore elaborated on by later writers, particularly in order to explain political arrangements among the twelve tribes generations after the Conquest. But even if one follows the inclination of some contemporary commentators to see an historical kernel in many of these tales, it is obvious that, in contrast to our examples from Judges and the David story, the authors, writing several centuries after the supposed events, had scant historical data to work with. To what degree they believed that the various traditions they inherited were actually historical is by no means clear, but if caution may deter us from applying a term like "invention" to their activity, it still seems likely that they exercised a good deal of shaping power over their materials as they articulated them. The point I should like to stress is that the immemorial inventions, fabrications, or projections of folk tradition are not in themselves fiction, which depends on the particularizing imagination of the individual writer. The authors of the Patriarchal narratives exhibit just such an imagination, transforming archetypal plots into the dramatic interaction of complex, probingly rendered characters. These stories

9. The pun has been observed by Luis Alonso-Schökel, who also comments on the play of ʿēgel in Eglon's name, "Erzählkunst im Buche der Richter," *Biblica* 42 (1961), 148–58.

are "historicized" both because they are presented as having a minute causal relation to known historical circumstances and because (as Schneidau argues) they have some of the irregular, "metonymic" quality of real historical concatenation; they are fiction because the national archetypes have been made to assume the distinctive lineaments of individual human lives.

Biblical narrative in fact offers a particularly instructive instance of the birth of fiction because it often exhibits the most arresting transitions from generalized statement, genealogical lists, mere summaries of characters and acts, to defined scene and concrete interaction between personages. Through the sudden specification of narrative detail and the invention of dialogue that individualizes the characters and focuses their relations, the biblical writers give the events they report a fictional time and place.

Let us consider a single succinct example, Esau's selling of the birthright to Jacob (Genesis 25):

> 27. As the lads grew up, Esau became a skilled hunter, a man of the field, and Jacob was a mild man, who kept to his tents. 28. Isaac loved Esau because he had a taste for game, but Rebekah loved Jacob. 29. Once when Jacob was cooking a stew, Esau came in from the field, famished. 30. Esau said to Jacob, "O, give me a swallow of this red red stuff for I am famished."—Thus is his name called Edom. 31. Jacob said, "First sell your birthright to me." 32. And Esau said, "Look, I am at the point of death, so what good to me is a birthright?" 33. And Jacob said, "Swear to me first," and he swore to him and sold his birthright to Jacob. 34. Then Jacob gave Esau bread and lentil stew, and he ate and he drank and he rose and he went off and Esau spurned the birthright.

Now Esau or Edom and Jacob or Israel are the eponymous founders of two neighboring and rival peoples, as the text has just forcefully reminded us in the oracle preceding their birth ("Two nations are in your womb./Two peoples apart while still in your belly./One people will outdo the other,/The older will serve the younger"). The story of the two rival brothers virtually asks us to read it as a political allegory, to construe each of the twins as an embodiment of his descendants' national characteristics, and to understand the course of their struggle as an outline of their future national destinies. The ruddy Esau, hungry for the red stew, is the progenitor of Edom, by folk etymology associated with *ʾādōm*, red, so that the people is given a kind of national emblem linked here with animality and gross appetite. This negative characterization is probably sharpened, as E. A. Speiser has proposed, by a borrowing from Near Eastern literary tradition: the red Esau, born with "a mantle of hair all over," would appear to allude to Enkidu of the Akkadian Gilgamesh Epic, whose birth is described in just this manner, and who is also an uncouth man of the field.[10] What happens, however, when the story is read entirely as a collision of national archetypes is strikingly illustrated by the commentaries of the early rabbis who—tending to interpret Edom as the typological forerunner of Rome—are relentless in making Esau out to be a vicious brute, while Jacob the tent-dweller becomes the model of pious Israel pondering the intricacies of God's revelation in the study of the Law. The anachronism of such readings concerns us less than the way they project onto the text, from their national-historical viewpoint, a neat moral polarity between the brothers. The text itself, conceiving its personages in

10. *The Anchor Bible: Genesis* (Garden City, New York, 1964), p. 196.

the fullness of a mature fictional imagination, presents matters rather differently, as even this brief passage from the larger Jacob-Esau story will suggest.

The episode begins with a schematic enough contrast between Esau the hunter and the sedentary Jacob. This apparently neat opposition, however, contains a lurking possibility of irony in the odd epithet *tām* attached to Jacob. Most translators have rendered it, as I have, by following the immediate context, and so have proposed something like "mild," "plain," or even "retiring" as an English equivalent. Perhaps this was in fact one recognized meaning of the term, but it should be noted that *all* the other biblical occurrences of the word—and it is frequently used, both in adjectival and nominative forms—refer to innocence or moral integrity. A little earlier in Genesis (20:5, 6) Abimelek professed the "innocence of his heart" (*tom-lēbāb*); in contrast to this collocation, Jeremiah, using the same verbal root that Esau sees in Jacob's name as an etymological signature of his treachery, will announce (17:9) that the "heart is treacherous" (*ʿāqōb hallēb*), a usage which opens the possibility that we are dealing here with recognized antonyms, both of them commonly bound in idiomatic compounds to the word for "heart." Jacob, *Yaʿăqōb*, whose name will soon be interpreted as "the one who deceives," is about to carry out an act if not of deception at least of shrewd calculation, and the choice of an epithet suggesting innocence as an introduction to the episode is bound to give us pause, to make us puzzle over the moral nature of Jacob—an enigma we shall still be trying to fathom twenty chapters later when he is an old man worn by experience, at last reunited with his lost son Joseph and received in the court of Pharaoh.

The next verse (28) provides an almost diagrammatic illustration of the Bible's artful procedure of variously stipulating or suppressing motive in order to elicit moral inferences and to suggest certain ambiguities. Isaac's preference for Esau is given a causal explanation so specific that it verges on satire: he loves the older twin because of his own fondness for game. Rebekah's love for Jacob is contrastively stated without explanation. Presumably, this would suggest that her affection is not dependent on a merely material convenience that the son might provide her, that it is a more justly grounded preference. Rebekah's maternal solicitude, however, is not without its troubling side, for we shall soon see a passive and rather timid Jacob briskly maneuvered about by his mother so that he will receive Isaac's blessing. This brief statement, then, of paternal preferences is both an interesting characterization of husband and wife and an effectively reticent piece of exposition in the story of the two brothers.

The twins then spring to life as fictional characters when the narration moves into dialogue (verses 30–33). Biblical Hebrew, as far as we can tell, does not incorporate in direct speech different levels of diction, deviations from standard grammar, regional or class dialects; but the writers, even in putting "normative" Hebrew in the mouths of all their personages, find ways of differentiating spoken language according to character. Esau asks for the stew with a verb used for the feeding of animals—one might suggest the force of the locution in English by rendering it as "let me cram my maw"—and, all inarticulate appetite, he cannot even think of the word for stew but only points to it pantingly as "this red red stuff." His explanation, however, "for I am famished," is factually precise, as it echoes verbatim what the narrator has just told us. In the first instance, that is, Esau does not choose an exaggeration, like that of verse 32, but states his actual condition: a creature of appetite, he is caught by the pangs of a terrible appetite. Esau speaks over the rumble of a growling stomach with the whiff of the cooking

stew in his nostrils. Jacob speaks with a clear perception of legal forms and future consequences, addressing his brother twice in the imperative—"First sell . . . swear to me
first"—without the deferential particle of entreaty, *nā*ᵓ, that Esau used in his own first
words to his twin. When Jacob asks Esau to sell the birthright, he withholds the crucial
"to me" till the end of his proposal with cautious rhetorical calculation. Fortunately for
him, Esau is too absorbed in his own immediate anguish—"I am at the point of
death"—to pay much attention to Jacob's self-interest. After the transaction is com-
pleted, as we move back from dialogue to uninterrupted narration, Esau's precipitous
character is mirrored stylistically in the rapid chain of verbs—"and he ate and he drank
and he rose and he went off"—that indicates the uncouth dispatch with which he
"spurned," or held in contempt, his birthright.

What is one to make of this vivid fictional realization of the scene in regard to its evident national-historical signification? The two are not really at cross-purposes, but certain complications of meaning are introduced in the process of fictional representation.
Esau, the episode makes clear, is not spiritually fit to be the vehicle of divine election,
the bearer of the birthright of Abraham's seed. He is altogether too much the slave of
the moment and of the body's tyranny to become the progenitor of the people promised
by divine covenant that it will have a vast historical destiny to fulfill. His selling of the
birthright in the circumstances here described is in itself proof that he is not worthy to
retain the birthright.

As the author, however, concretely imagines Jacob, what emerges from the scene is
more than simple Israelite (and anti-Edomite) apologetics. Jacob is a man who thinks
about the future, indeed, who often seems worried about the future, and we shall
repeatedly see him making prudent stipulations in legal or quasi-legal terms, with God,
with Laban, with the divine messenger, about future circumstances. This qualifies him
as a suitable bearer of the birthright: historical destiny does not just happen; you have
to know how to make it happen, how to keep your eye on the distant horizon of present
events. But this quality of wary calculation does not necessarily make Jacob more appealing as a character, and, indeed, may even raise some moral questions about him.
The contrast in our scene between the impetuous, miserably famished Esau and the
shrewdly businesslike Jacob may not be entirely to Jacob's advantage, and the episode is
surely a little troubling as an instance of the quality of "innocence" which the narrator
has just fastened as an epithet to the younger twin. His subsequent stealing of his blind
father's blessing by pretending to be Esau (chapter 27) sets him in a still more am-
biguous light; and this judgment that Jacob has done wrong in taking what is in a sense
his is later confirmed in the narrative, as Umberto Cassuto and other commentators
have noted: Jacob becomes the victim of symmetrical poetic justice, deceived in the
blindness of the night by having Leah passed off on him as Rachel, and rebuked in the
morning by the deceiver, his father-in-law Laban—"It is not done thus in our region to
give the younger daughter before the firstborn" (29:26).

If one insists on seeing the Patriarchal narratives strictly as paradigms for later
Israelite history, one would have to conclude that the authors and redactor of the Jacob
story were political subversives raising oblique but damaging questions about the national enterprise. Actually, there may be some theological warrant for this introduction
of ambiguities into the story of Israel's eponymous hero, for in the perspective of ethical
monotheism, covenantal privileges by no means automatically confer moral perfection,
and that monitory idea is perhaps something the writers wanted to bring to the attention

of their audiences. I do not think, though, that every nuance of characterization and every turning of the plot in these stories can be justified in either moral-theological or national-historical terms. Perhaps this is the ultimate difference between any hermaneutic approach to the Bible and the literary approach that I am proposing: in the hermaneutic perspective, the text exhibits a kind of absolute functionalism, all its detectable features serving some purpose in a semantics of the holy; in the literary perspective, there is latitude for the exercise of pleasurable invention for its own sake, ranging from "microscopic" details like sound-play to macroscopic features like the psychology of individual characters.

This need not imply a blurring of necessary distinctions between sacred and secular literature. The biblical authors are of course constantly, urgently conscious of telling a story in order to reveal the imperative truth of God's works in history and of Israel's hopes and failings. Close attention to the literary strategies through which that truth was expressed may actually help us to understand it better, enable us to see the minute elements of complicating design in the Bible's sacred history. But it also seems to me important to emphasize that the operation of the literary imagination develops a momentum of its own, even for a tradition of writers as theologically intent as these. Genesis is not *Pale Fire*, but fiction, including the Bible, is in some sense a form of play. Play in the sense I have in mind enlarges rather than limits the range of meanings of the text. For the classics of fiction, ancient and modern, embody in a vast variety of modes the most serious playfulness, endlessly discovering how the permutations of narrative conventions, linguistic properties, and imaginatively constructed personages and circumstances can crystallize subtle and abiding truths of experience in amusing or arresting or gratifying ways. The Bible presents a kind of literature in which the primary impulse would often seem to be to provide instruction or at least necessary information, not merely to delight. If, however, we fail to see that the creators of biblical narrative were writers who, like writers elsewhere, took pleasure in exploring the formal and imaginative resources of their fictional medium, perhaps sometimes unexpectedly capturing the fullness of their subject in the very play of exploration, we shall miss much that the biblical stories are meant to convey.

Sacred History and Theology:
The Redaction of Torah

RICHARD ELLIOTT FRIEDMAN

One of the significant consequences of the enterprise of source criticism is the demonstration that the Torah (and ultimately the Hebrew Bible), more than perhaps any other book, is the product of a community—it is quintessentially a national work of literature, not the creation of a particular man or woman in a particular historical moment, but the offspring of a continuing, developing culture.

A more troubling consequence of the source-critical enterprise is the difficulty it engenders when one returns from it to the reading and studying of the whole. Thus is born redaction criticism, the study of the final literary product which we call Torah with the sophistication of one who knows something of the complex literary history of the text. The focus now is upon the literary figure who assembled the received texts into a single work. The combinatory design which this redactor conceived did more than house the received texts. It gave birth to new narrative syntheses.

Martin Noth wrote that, precisely because the Priestly source (P) depended upon the JE sources (or because both depended upon a common *Grundlage*), the combination of P and JE did not result in any major new element, historical or theological, in the unified work.[1] I believe, however, that we may perceive several significant metamorphoses in the conception of God and in the portrayal of the *magnalia Dei* which result from the design of the Priestly tradent who was responsible for the redaction of the work.[2]

The juxtaposition of the J and Priestly Creation accounts, first, precipitated a narrative synthesis with exegetical possibilities which neither of the original documents possessed independently. The humans who reach to the Tree of Knowledge of Good and Evil are different from all other creatures in that they bear the stamp of the *imago Dei*. Without pursuing the precise meaning of *ṣelem* and *dᵊmût*, one can say at minimum that humans are portrayed as embodying some divine element—and this element is

---

1. "Partly in consequence of a common harking back to a fully developed oral narrative tradition, and partly in consequence of mutual literary dependence, the course of history was narrated so much the same in all the sources that even their combination with one another could change nothing essential in this regard." Noth, *A History of Pentateuchal Traditions* (Englewood Cliffs, New Jersey, 1972), 250; German edition, *Überlieferungsgeschichte des Pentateuch* (1948).

2. I use the term *tradent* to denote one who is both editor and writer, one whose handling of received texts involves both arrangement and elaboration. I have elsewhere described his task and identified the texts which are to be ascribed to him: R. E. Friedman, *The Exile and Biblical Narrative* (Harvard Semitic Monographs 22, Chico, Calif., 1981). Following F. M. Cross, I identify him as Priestly and refer to his final product (which includes at least the Tetrateuch, and possibly Deuteronomy as well) as the Priestly work.

critical to the events of Eden. Insofar as beings who share some quality with Yhwh are nonetheless treated by him as his subordinates, his communication with them being initially and nearly exclusively commands, the stage is set for their disobedience even before the introduction of the serpent as catalyst. When Mark Twain queried, "If the Lord didn't want humans to be rebellious then why did he create them in his image?" he was at his theologically ironic best. Depicted as creating humans in his own image and then setting under prohibition the fruit whose very attraction is to endow one with a divine power, Yhwh is thus portrayed as himself creating the terms of that tension which results in human disobedience. Themselves possessing some godly quality, the humans are attracted precisely by the serpent's claim that if they eat from the tree they will be like God(s). This tension, however, is neither the work of the author of J nor the work of the Priestly author. It is purely a by-product of the combination of the two at the hand of the tradent. P does not portray a primal human rebellion; J does not portray the creation of humans in the image of God. The combination of these two re-cast the interpretive range of the motive of the humans' actions in Eden. In the final product we call Torah, one cannot separate the creation *in imago Dei* from the natures of the humans who disobey the divine instruction. Interestingly, Noth referred to this identification of the humans who are created in the divine image with the humans who rebel, but he concluded only that the combined text thus accurately reflects a condition of humankind, while he held nonetheless that this effect of combination of texts still constitutes no new narrative or theological component of the whole.[3] In response, I would insist that the effect of the combination of these originally alternative texts was profound—in this case refocusing the perspective of the first chapters of the biblical narrative. Indeed, insofar as the struggle between Yhwh and the human community persists as an obvious and dominant theme in biblical narrative, the Genesis 1–3 account of the archetype of that struggle sets a fundamental *Leitmotif* of those narratives. From this perspective, it is difficult to overestimate the impact of the tradent who produced in Genesis 1–3 a narrative which is quite literally more than the sum of its components.

One may observe a broader metamorphosis in the portrayal of Yhwh in the unified Priestly work when one compares certain features of the JE and Priestly theologies. It is regularly noted in theological studies of the Hebrew Bible that one finds in P a more cosmic perspective of Yhwh than in the other sources.[4] Specifically, one observes, first, that the Sabbath is fixed in the orders of Creation in P, while it is not in J, and functions as commemorative of historical national events in D. Second, the Priestly Creation account depicts the construction of the entire universe, describing a "cosmic bubble" of sky over earth with water above and below, while the J Creation focuses exclusively on the earth and the birth of plant and animal life thereon, with Yhwh personally moving about among his creatures. Interestingly, the Priestly narrative begins: "When God began to create *the heavens and the earth*" (Gen 1:1), while J begins, "In the day that Yhwh God made *earth and heaven*" (2:4b). The reversed order, as it happens, is appropriate to the respective points of view, as E. A. Speiser has observed.[5] Again in the

---

3. Noth, *History*, 251.

4. E.g., Gerhard von Rad, *Old Testament Theology*, 1 (New York, 1962), 148f. (German edition, *Theologie des Alten Testaments*, 1957); E. A. Speiser, *Genesis: The Anchor Bible* (Garden City, New York, 1964), xxvff.

5. Speiser, *Genesis*, 18f.

Flood account, P portrays a cosmic crisis in which the habitable bubble is threatened; the fountains of the deep are divided, thus causing the waters to flow up from below; and the windows of heaven are divided, thus causing the waters to flow down from above. The J version meanwhile merely reports rain. P, further, adds the Noahic covenant to those of JE tradition (the Abrahamic and Israelite covenants), thus setting the latter covenants, which bind Yhwh to a particular community of humans, into a larger framework of a covenant with all flesh. In all of these instances the Priestly writer portrays Yhwh in conceptually broader terms than those of the JE portrayal. The Priestly compositions consistently desist from the angelic and blatantly anthropomorphic portrayals which are widespread in JE tradition. In the Priestly portrayal of history there is never an appearance of an angel. There is never a portrayal of Yhwh so anthropomorphic as the JE portrayals of Yhwh's walking in the Garden, standing on a rock in the wilderness, wrestling with Jacob, making Adam's and Eve's loincloths, and closing Noah's ark. There is never a talking animal. There is never a dream narrative. It is no oversimplification to characterize P as a more clearly cosmic portrayal of the deity, and JE as a more personal conception. But, again, the merging of the two portrayals in the unified work of the Priestly tradent yielded a new formula, i.e., a synthesis in which the cosmic and the personal aspects of God stood in a balance unlike that of either of the component compositions. It is this theological synthesis, in which Yhwh appears as both universal and personal, as both the Creator and "the God of your father," that has seeded Jewish and Christian conceptions of God for millennia. Yet it was neither the conception of JE nor of P—but, rather, something new, a product of the union of the two at the hand of the Priestly tradent.

A second synthetic theological formulation was born in the unified Priestly work with regard to the portrayal of the mercy of Yhwh. The centrality of the mercy of Yhwh to JE tradition is manifest in the divine formula revealed to Moses on Sinai in Exod 34:6f. Yhwh is "merciful and gracious, long-forbearing and abundant in *ḥesed*. . . . " It is upon this formula that Moses bases his appeal that Yhwh rescind his condemnation of the nation following the spy incident in Num 14:13-20. The appeal is successful, as is Moses' prior appeal following a similar condemnation in the golden calf incident (Exod 32:11-14). Israel's God, in JE portrayal, is a deity who can be "grieved to his heart" by the actions of his humans (Gen 6:6). The well-known compassion of Yhwh, which is responsible for innumerable reprieves for Israel's continual violations of covenant in JE and Deuteronomistic literature—and which pervades the Psalms and Prophetic literature—is, however, almost entirely unknown in P. The fundamental vocabulary of the category of mercy, formalized in the divine formula of Exodus 34, is completely missing in the Priestly compositions. All forms of the root *rḥm* are missing, as are all forms of *ḥnn*.[6] There is not a single reference to the *ḥesed* of Yhwh.[7] The regular biblical term for repentance, *šwb*, never appears in P, as Jacob Milgrom has observed.[8] Not only is the terminology of divine mercy absent in P, but the portrayal of it as a phenomenon in narrative is exceedingly rare as well. Notably, Moses' appeal for mercy

---

6. The second element of the threefold Priestly blessing, Num 6:25, is the lone possible exception to the absence of the root *ḥnn*, but this passage may be Exilic, i.e., the addition of the tradent himself, and in any event is almost certainly the insertion of an actual formal cultic ceremony, not narrative composition.

7. The mention of *ḥesed* in the Decalogue is common to the Exodus 20 and Deuteronomy 5 versions and is clearly related to the Exodus 34 formula. It is therefore not original to P.

8. *Cult and Conscience* (Leiden, 1976), 121ff.

in the matter of the spies in JE is simply eliminated in the Priestly version of that episode. In P, instead of Yhwh's sentence being made more lenient as a result of the arguments of Moses, the sentence is simply pronounced and carried out. The similar appeal of Moses in the matter of the golden calf in JE of course has no counterpart in P—the latter, being the product of the Aaronid priesthood, eliminated the story of the golden calf, in which the eponymous ancestor of the Aaronids figured centrally as culpable in the incident.

This reduced concern with mercy, grace, *ḥesed*, and repentance in P is itself a valuable datum for exegesis, and for dating as well.[9] My present concern, however, is specifically to note the effect of the combination of the differing compositions. Quite simply, the uniting of the JE and Priestly texts within the single Priestly work resulted in a new theological formula of justice and mercy which corresponded neither to that of JE nor to that of P. The proportional ratio of these qualities to one another within the character of Yhwh in the Priestly work bore no resemblance to that of either of its components. The portrayal of Yhwh in the united Torah therefore depicts the deity as embodying a quality of compassion which the Priestly writer(s) never intended to emphasize so, while it develops the reverse constituent of the divine character far beyond the original portrayal thereof in JE texts. A new view of the tension between the divine traits of mercy and justice was thus born in the design of the Priestly tradent.

The enterprise of the Priestly tradent thus resulted in a Torah whose theology was neither independent of its sources nor a simple composite of them. We have seen three examples of the impact of this literary process upon the component texts which have significant theological implications. The question is whether this phenomenon of narrative metamorphosis through combination is the chance result of the mechanical combination of the sources, of interest now primarily to a sociologist or cultural anthropologist as reflecting layers of a culture—or can we pursue the intention of the redactor and uncover and identify a theological consciousness.

Initial study of the text would lead one to believe that the tradent's redactional decisions in combining and arranging his sources were motivated primarily by mechanical considerations. In the narrative of the Flood, for example, each of the two accounts which we have, J and P, when separated from one another, constitutes a complete, flowing account of the Flood event. The Priestly tradent's method clearly was to segment the two versions and to place the thematically corresponding blocks adjacent to one another: e.g., entrance into the ark, initiation of the deluge, expiration of living creatures, recession of water, dispatching of birds, etc. The redactional design here does not seem to be theologically motivated, but, rather, the product of a literary mechanical decision. The same goes for the Red Sea narrative, in which at least the P and J accounts (though not the E) are each independently complete, flowing stories and are combined in a brilliant synthesis in which the differing versions are united in an incomparably unified continuous narrative. Here, especially, the redactional genius seems to be mechanical rather than theological or ideological. The episode of the spies in the Book of Numbers reflects the same *modus operandi*: two accounts, each a complete, fluent story, segmented and combined with adjacent juxtaposition of thematically corresponding blocks. In each of these three cases—the Flood, the Sea, the spies—the

9. If P were Exilic, the absence of any reference to repentance or to divine mercy would be strange indeed.

natural mechanics of the process of redaction are sufficient to explain the combinatory constructions before us.

A variation of this technique is segmentation and distribution. The Priestly version of the Abraham/Lot sequence of events, for example, is an abbreviated account (merely four verses long; Gen 12:5; 13:6, 11b, 12a; 19:29). When separated from the JE materials (12:4, 6-20; 13:1-11a, 12b-18; 18:1-33; 19:1-38) these four verses flow comfortably as a unit, a summary version of the longer JE narrative. The redactor, patently, has segmented this unit and distributed the pieces over eight chapters of Genesis in thematically appropriate junctures. The result of this segmentation and distribution design was that the redactor was able to retain this Priestly material without contradicting the narrative sequence of events in the JE texts. The same redactional process seems to have been in operation in the handling of the Jacob/Esau materials and of the accounts of the migration and settlement of the Israelites in Egypt. In each of these cases we have a short Priestly narrative, complete or nearly so in itself, segmented and distributed through a larger body of narrative material at thematically satisfactory junctures.[10] In all three cases, again, the design before us is an editorial mechanism, demonstrably a response to the mechanical requirements of this redactor's unique enterprise.

If we focus upon smaller pericopes in a more specific way, the case becomes even clearer. In the account of the Patriarchal migration from Mesopotamia, for example, we have both a Priestly and a J account of the event. The Priestly account portrays the migration in two stages: namely, Terah brings the family from Ur to Haran; Abram brings the family from Haran to Canaan. The J material contains only the command of God to Abram to leave his birthplace, followed by the report that Abram did as God had commanded him. (P: Gen 11:31, 12:4b, 5; J: 12:1-a) The tradent who received these two texts did not choose to set the P text before the J, nor the J before the P, nor to eliminate one or the other. He rather chose to combine them by having the J narrative intersect the two stages of the Priestly record. Thus in our Torah we read that Terah brings the family to Haran, then Yhwh commands Abram *lēk l³kā*, then Abram brings the family to Canaan. This arrangement is mechanically mandated. The Priestly account of the Terah-led migration (with Terah "taking" the family) had to precede the J divine command to Abram to migrate. The J divine command to Abram to migrate had to precede the Priestly account of the Abram-led migration (with Abram "taking" the family). One may object that the present arrangement still has a structural problem in that as it now stands Abram is being told (12:1) to leave his birthplace (*mwldtk*), but his birthplace is back in Ur, and he is already in Haran! Indeed, Rashi, Ibn Ezra, and Ramban raise this very question and propose the most complex models of migration to reconcile the facts. Such a problem, however, is a constant, for if the tradent had chosen to set the J narrative wholly before that of P, the problem of "Leave your birthplace" would have been solved, but a problem of "Leave your father's house (*mbyt ³byk*)" would then be born, because Abram's being taken by Terah would then look even clumsier than we observed earlier.[11] To have set the J version wholly after that of P

---

10. The Priestly Jacob/Esau account: Gen 26:34f.; 27:46; 281-9. The Priestly migration account: Gen 37:1; 41:45b, 46a; 46:6, 7; 47:27b.

11. The objection is questionable in any event since the term *mwldtk* has a broader range of meaning than

would be less credible still, for then Abram would already have left home prior to the divine command to *lēk ləkā*. In short, the redactional design of our united text is based on factors of the mechanics of the literary construction.

The redaction of the Abrahamic covenant traditions likewise reflects decisions grounded in the mechanics of literary combination. In this case the redactor placed the J version (Genesis 15) before that of P (Genesis 17) and separated the two by placing the J and P accounts of Hagar and the birth of Ishmael between them. The arrangement reflects the requirements of the received texts. In the J tradition, the Abrahamic covenant precedes the birth of Ishmael; and the wording of the J text holds the redactor to maintaining the integrity of this tradition, for in the text Abraham remarks that he is childless (*hōlēk ʿărîrî*; 15:2). Priestly tradition, however, specifically develops the notion that Ishmael is already born prior to the inception of the hereditary covenant, but God rejects Abraham's appeal for Ishmael as covenantal heir and announces the forthcoming birth of Isaac (17:18f). Thus this text, too, holds the redactor to its integrity. The result: the Torah as we have it.

The account of the divine acquaintance and commission to Moses is a third example of this redactional activity. The J charge to Moses, set at the burning bush, includes the divine assurance that when Moses goes to the people in Egypt they will listen to him (Exod 3:18). Exodus 4 then concludes with the notation that the people do listen (4:31). In the Priestly version of the commission (which does not identify the place in which it occurs) Yhwh sends Moses to the people with the announcement of imminent rescue, and the text specifically notes: "But they did *not* listen . . . " (6:9). The Priestly tradent, thus confronted with a contradictive doublet, introduced the Priestly text of the charge to Moses following the J account of Moses' *second* meeting with the leaders of the people. In the tradent's design, as it now stands, God charges Moses in Midian, Moses goes to the people in Egypt and announces the coming liberation, the people listen, Moses' first exchange with Pharaoh results in increased burdens upon the people, the leaders of the people express their anger to Moses—then, following this second, unsatisfactory encounter with the people, comes the Priestly text: God charges Moses to go to the people with an announcement of liberation, and the people do not listen.

Through these several cases, the method of the redactor begins to be apparent, as follows: he apparently tried to retain as much of the received material as possible, this balanced against the editorial considerations of producing a narrative which, *for him*, had sufficient unity and sense. He was not bound to any one fixed design, but rather he might place two complete narratives side by side, or intersect one with the other, or relocate one or the other, or use segmentation and thematic combination or distribution. Finally, he united the whole within two editorial frameworks, themselves derived from received texts, as Frank Cross has described.[12] Cross identified the first of these as the *ʾelleh tôlədōt* series of headings, a genealogical framework derived from a "*tôlədōt* Book," which provided a continuity for the collected narrative materials in the book of Genesis. The second such framework was the "Wilderness Stations" series of headings, an itinerary framework derived from the Numbers 33 list of Israel's movements during

merely "birthplace." See, e.g., Esth 2:10, and S. Talmon's treatment in "The Textual Study of the Bible—A New Outlook," in F. M. Cross and S. Talmon, eds., *Qumran and the History of the Biblical Text* (Cambridge, Massachusetts, 1975), 360.

12. *Canaanite Myth and Hebrew Epic* (Cambridge, Massachusetts, 1973), 301-317.

the forty years' wilderness journey, which provided a continuity for the narrative and legal materials from Exodus 12 through the arrival of Israel at the Plains of Moab in the Book of Numbers.

In all of the material which I have noted here, mechanical considerations are a sufficient explanation of the redactional design. In several of the cases, mechanical considerations are a necessary explanation. Still we must be hesitant to pronounce the redactor's task to be wholly grounded in editorial mechanics. Where this is a sufficient explanation, we must be open to the possibility of theological or ideological redactional motives which are no less sufficient explanations. And even in those cases in which mechanical considerations are so patent as to compel us to acknowledge their determinism of the redactor's decisions in these pericopes, this is not to say that the redactor was an unthinking creature who was not sensitive to the literary implications—theological or others—of his designs. I therefore seek evidence of the presence of a theological consciousness on the part of the Priestly tradent who redacted the Torah.

One narrative in particular points to the existence of such a theological consciousness, namely, the plagues narrative of the Book of Exodus. Brevard Childs, Moshe Greenberg, and Ziony Zevit have observed that in the plagues traditions J and P do not stand in tension but are bound together to form a richer narrative.[13] The plagues traditions of Exodus form one of the most complex constructions of Priestly and JE composition in the Torah. Separated from one another, neither JE nor the Priestly material flows comfortably. As Cross has pointed out, it is hardly possible to picture the present shape of the section as the basically mechanical juxtaposition of corresponding blocks of two narratives by a redactor.[14] Upon examination one finds that this construction is a special design of the tradent who produced the unified Priestly work. In the plagues narrative one may uncover an editorial framework which, like the *tôlᵊdōt* and Stations frameworks which respectively precede and follow it, gives shape to the materials which it encloses, thus accounting for what is otherwise a thirteen-chapter gap between the two structures which Cross identified. Just as the *tôlᵊdōt* and Stations frameworks are based on received texts which the tradent had at his disposal, so the framework of the plagues section is derivative from a received text, namely, the Priestly account of Moses and Pharaoh. In this account, Yhwh informs Moses prior to the latter's first meeting with Pharaoh that "I shall harden Pharaoh's heart . . . and he will not listen to you" (Exod 7:3f). The realization of this prediction is then noted several times in the account of Moses and Pharaoh which follows. Using the verbs *qšh* and *ḥzq* for "to harden," this is the Priestly alternative to the JE account, which regularly uses the verb *kbd* for the hardening of Pharoah's heart. The latter is consistent with a regular play upon the term *kābēd* in the JE account. Moses is *kᵊbad lāšôn ûkᵊbad peh* (literally, "hard of tongue and hard of mouth"), while Pharaoh is *kᵊbad lēb* ("hard of heart"). After his first meeting with Moses, Pharaoh declares, *tikbad haʿăbōdāh* ("let the work be hard"; 5:9). Moses predicts *deber kābēd* ("hard pestilence"; 9:3). There falls *bārād kābēd* ("hard hail"; 9:24).

13. Childs, *The Book of Exodus* (Philadelphia, 1974), 155; Zevit, "The Priestly Redaction and Interpretation of the Plague Narrative in Exodus," *JQR* 66 (1976), 199; Greenberg, "The Redaction of the Plague Narrative in Exodus," *Near Eastern Studies in Honor of William Foxwell Albright*, ed., H. Goedicke (Baltimore, 1971), 243-252.

14. Cross, *Canaanite Myth*, 318.

The difference between the JE and Priestly portrayals of the hardening of Pharaoh's heart, though, is more than one of terminology. The JE account is a confrontation in which the personality of Pharaoh, his strengths and his weaknesses, figures integrally in the dynamic. Pharaoh is a thinking, arguing, *deciding* character. It is Pharaoh himself who makes his heart hard. Pharaoh several times agrees to liberate the people if only the current plague will cease, but upon seeing respite hardens his heart. He bargains with Moses several times over the terms of the liberation. The focus is upon his (Pharaoh's) decision. At the burning bush, God informs Moses: "I know that the king of Egypt will not *permit* you to go . . . " (Exod 3:19), claiming only precognition of Pharaoh's will, not divine determination. Moses continually speaks to Pharaoh in a manner which suggests volition on the king's part: "How long will you refuse . . . ?" (7:27; 8:17; 9:2, 17f.; 10:3f.); and God himself says to Moses: "The heart of Pharaoh is hard, he refuses to send forth the people" (7:14), suggesting only *knowledge* of the condition of Pharaoh's will, not control. Only once does the text associate the power of God with the hardening of Pharaoh's heart. In Exod 10:1, after five plagues have already occurred in the JE narrative, Yhwh tells Moses: "*I* have hardened his heart. . . ." So anomalous is this statement compared to all that which precedes it and follows it in the JE plagues account that it is widely held among scholars that this verse and the one following must be a secondary insertion. Even if we do not call for a gloss here, though, we must at minimum see this passage as a surprising turn from the rest of the text, never developed further by the author, albeit perhaps intentionally.

The Priestly story of the plagues, however, carries this notion to divine control of Pharaoh's will full-blown. As we have already observed, in the Priestly version God informs Moses at the outset that *he* will harden Pharaoh's heart. In P, further, Pharaoh has no dialogue; he makes no promises of liberation and no reversals. Whereas in JE it is apparently the respite from plagues itself that makes Pharaoh harden his heart, no such action appears in P, where the development is rather a fast crescendo: in the plagues of blood and frogs the Egyptian magicians duplicate the wonders; in the plague of lice the magicians fail to duplicate it, and they say, "it is the finger of God"; in the plague of boils, the magicians are themselves afflicted. But the developing divine victory, from which no respite is mentioned, does not turn Pharaoh's thinking around, because Yhwh has predetermined to *harden Pharaoh's heart*.

Examination of each of the appearances of this notation clarifies for us the redactional design which the Priestly tradent constructed to house these materials.

The episode of Aaron's rod becoming a snake (P) concludes with the prediction-fulfilling Priestly notation, "And the heart of Pharaoh was hard (*wyḥzq*), and he did not listen to them, as Yhwh had said" (7:13). The description of the blood plague (P and JE combined) concludes identically (7:22). The description of the plague of frogs (P and JE combined) ends with the JE notation that Pharoah hardened (*hkbd*) his heart (8:11), but attached to this JE statement is the Priestly remainder: " . . . and he did not listen to them, as Yhwh had said." The plagues of lice and boils (both wholly P) conclude with the full Priestly statement (8:15; 9:12). The plagues of flies and pestilence (both wholly JE) each conclude with the full JE statement: "And Pharaoh hardened (*wkybd*) his heart, and he did not send forth the people" (8:28; 9:7). Thus the plague accounts which are wholly P conclude with the P notation, those which are wholly JE conclude with the JE notation, and those which are combined conclude with the P notation or with a combined notation. This unsurprising picture changes, however, in the remaining plagues. The plague of hail is entirely a JE composition, yet it concludes with a mixed notation in which the Priestly elements predominate, thus: "And the heart of Pharaoh was hard (*wyḥzq*), and he did not send forth the children of Israel, as Yhwh had said" (9:35). A Priestly statement has somehow come to summarize a JE pericope.[15] The lengthy narrative which follows, climaxing in the plague of locusts, likewise is wholly JE, but concludes: "And Yhwh hardened (*wyḥzq*) the heart of Pharaoh, and he did not send forth the people" (10:20). The account of the plague of darkness follows; it, too, is entirely a JE composition, yet it concludes similarly to the two preceding accounts (10:27). There follows a JE portrayal of the last dialogue of Moses and Pharaoh, at the end of which stands a Priestly conclusion to the entire sequence of Moses/Pharaoh encounters, thus:

> And Moses and Aaron performed all these wonders before Pharaoh, and Yhwh hardened (*wyḥzq*) the heart of Pharaoh, and he did not send forth the children of Israel from his land. (11:10)

The presence of Priestly conclusions upon JE narratives, fulfilling the prediction which is made in a Priestly introduction, and arriving finally at a Priestly summation, indicates that we have in the Exodus account of Moses and Pharaoh portions of two received texts, one P and one JE, which have been combined by the Priestly tradent in a framework which he modeled upon the P version. A final indicator that this is the case is the presence of the Priestly formulation of the hardening-of-the-heart phrase in the midst of the account of God's initial instructions to Moses (4:21b). The context is somewhat awkward as it stands (4:21–23) and apparently reflects the tradent's unifying work. Indeed, the specific combination of phrases in this verse (4:21b) viz., that God will harden (*ḥzq*) Pharaoh's heart and that Pharaoh will not send forth the people, otherwise occurs only in the four passages which we last observed.

The effect of this redactional design was to cause the Priestly notion of divine control of the chain of events to dominate the entire combined narrative. With the Priestly predictions that God would harden Pharaoh's heart now located at the beginning of the narrative, not only did the subsequent *Priestly* notations of this hardening portray fulfillment of this divine intention; now the *JE* expressions of hardening fell into this rubric as well. Every JE notation that Pharaoh hardened his heart now appeared to be the fulfillment of the original prediction, with the invisible power of Yhwh controlling Pharaoh's action. The JE picture of a confrontation between Pharaoh and the power of God in which the divine might proves victorious was now a part of a larger scheme in which the deity controls both sides of the dynamic, both Moses' challenge and Pharaoh's response.

Nothing of the redactional design which we have observed in the plagues narrative is critical to the mechanics of the combination of the texts. If we remove the references to God's hardening of Pharaoh's heart which I have identified as redactional additions, the narrative still flows continuously and sensibly. In this case the Priestly tradent has conceived a literary structure based on considerations other than purely mechanical

---

15. The distinction between *ḥzq* and *kbd* is consistently confirmed in the LXX. Note also the doublet of the hardening of Pharaoh's heart in 9:34 (*kbd*) and again in 9:35 (*ḥzq*). *ḥzq lb*, further, continues as a key term in P through the Sea episode, Exod 14:4, 8 (cf. v 5, JE), 17.

demands. He has not been governed by the character of the received texts to the extent that he was in the case of the Flood texts or the Abrahamic covenant texts. He has, rather, increased his share of the literary partnership between himself and the authors of his received texts. He has favored and developed a particular theological notion, he has imposed it upon the whole, and thus he has produced a united narrative which, like the united creation accounts, is more than the sum of its components. Even as God controls both sides of the confrontation, owing to the Priestly text and the derivative framework, it is still the thinking, struggling Pharaoh of the JE texts who is thus controlled. The combined portrayal thus magnifies the power of the God of Israel, who now exercises supreme determinism over a more worthy opponent. And this picture is not the chance by-product of mechanical editing. The nature of the design rather points to a theological consciousness on the part of the designer.

Thus, in addition to the retention of received materials and the fashioning of unified, sensible constructions, another factor enters the formula of the tradent's *modus operandi*, namely, the tradent's own theological sensitivities.

In any given pericope, these factors may stand in different balance. The theological considerations may play a significant part in the tradent's conception of the redactional design, or mechanical considerations may be determinative. Our task now is to analyze each narrative, independently and in context of the whole, to weigh with more particularity the balance of factors which motivated the tradent's design in each case: what did he perceive to be contradiction? Which contradictions were to him tolerable, and which did he perceive to require resolution? Ultimately, what was the nature and the extent of the Priestly tradent's contribution to the creation of the Torah? Even these early researches point to the likelihood that his contribution was no less significant and no less creative than that of the authors who, knowingly or not, bequeathed their work into his care.

Sacred History and Ideology: Chronicles' Thematic Structure — Indications of an Earlier Source

BARUCH HALPERN

A few years ago, at a Waltham, Massachusetts, computer firm, a PDP-10 system began rather suddenly to read out error-messages at random points in its operation. A program would run through smoothly once, twice, or ten times, but on the next run an error-message would slash it to a halt. If the program was sent through again, no hitch occurred.

The operators were baffled; they checked the switches. The programmers were stymied; they examined the programs and, later, when that produced nothing, the compiler and the very grammar of the machine language. Digital Equipment Corporation eventually dispatched its field service representatives. They dismantled the machine piece by piece and put it back together. They found nothing. The error-messages continued in their random way—appearing and vanishing like a Circuit Pimpernel. The situation lasted for weeks.

One day, one of the company's hardware specialists noticed that an electric cord behind a line printer was piled in a slightly tangled way. He kicked it. From that moment, the error-messages ceased. The hardware man had no inkling of any connection between the cord and the error-ticks. He was just kicking a wire. But it transpired subsequently that the minute impulses that penetrated the cord's insulation had influenced the memory banks to affect the line printer in such a way as to create the apparition of a perverse independent intelligence in the machine. Probably, if artificial intelligence ever is created, it will be by some such accident as this.

Good art, curiously, is in the position of that computer. In its programmed imitation of the organic, it should take on an artificial life of its own. This constitutes a present danger to the scholar: a biblicist who seeks to retroject that artificial life into the mind of the author or editor is in peril of confounding project with product.[1]

In essence, this problem is the one addressed in Richard Friedman's essay above. In a very different sense, it is the subject also of the essay by John Russiano Miles below. Simply, the literary approach to biblical texts is unquestionably valid where authorship is unitary. Where the question of authorship is more complex, other considerations intrude. The authorial theory now prevalent in biblical literary studies, or the converse New Critical view of intent, is a legitimate implement for construing texts from the

---

1. See, recently, E. D. Hirsch, Jr., *Validity in Interpretation* (New Haven, Connecticut, 1967), for a fairly balanced assessment of the problems involved.

modern viewpoint. For the historian—of Israel's religion, culture, ideas, or just of Israel—these are less useful. The biblical scholar who subscribes to the former[2] is potential prey to the intentional fallacy precisely where the fallacy is plainest—where the author is under compulsion to acknowledge or even to include materials either irrelevant or antithetic to his viewpoint.

In other words, the scholar is responsible to inquire, to what extent was the form of a work dictated by the use of sources, and to what extent the product of the redactor himself? How did the redactor use his sources, if any? How did he regard them? As canon? As true reports? Or as the fallible recollections of an imperfect journalist? Moreover, in what spirit did a redactor incorporate them? The models common today in scholarship—and to which I have myself on more than one occasion adhered—are far from being the only models on which to construe the redactorial enterprise. We are confronted with a phenomenon alien to us. It may be as complex as the Gordian knot—and it is not up to us to unravel it with a vorpal snickersnack. On the contrary, we are compelled to follow through each individual strand, until we recognize either a single, simple key, or the conglomerate, variegated nature of the problem.

The books of Chronicles and Kings, by virtue of being the only demonstrably synoptic and extensive historical works in the Bible, provide a unique testing-ground for source criticism. The only difficulty lies in the fact that the relationship between the two has not yet been fathomed. In the succeeding pages, therefore, I shall examine a specific but sprawling problem: does an extensive historical work underlie the present versions of Chronicles and Kings? In so doing, I mean to suggest that the model of redaction suggested by the evidence has relevance to "redaction" in all Israelite historiography (including the Pentateuch). Here, the only way to recover authorial intent is to judge, not just the final product, much less the material of which it was made, but the difference between the sculpture and the block.

I

The books of Chronicles first burst into full-blown narrative with a part of the story of Saul's death, taken from 1 Sam 31 (1 Chron 10). From this point to 1 Chron 21, Chronicles marches more or less through 2 Samuel, on which it seems to depend. However, in contrast to Samuel, where Saul's death represents the solution to a problem, the end of a certain narrative tension, Saul's death in Chronicles serves more the function of the primeval history in Genesis: it erects the problem to which David presents the solution:

"(Saul) did not seek Yhwh; so he killed him, and diverted the kingship to David ben-Yishai" (10:14).[3] At the outset, David's monarchy is recognized by Israel. He takes Jerusalem. Yhwh is with him, and his career is on the wax (11:9). This leads to a review of his followers, and those "who came to . . . Hebron to divert the kingship of Saul to (David)" (12:23). Immediately thereafter, David gathers all the people of Israel, from all the lands of Israel, and says, "Let us divert the ark of our god to us, for we did not

---

2. A case in point is H. G. M. Williamson, *Israel in the Books of Chronicles* (Cambridge, England, 1977).

3. See my *Constitution of the Monarchy in Israel* (Harvard Semitic Monograph, forthcoming), chap. 6, for a discussion of the bearings of the accounts of Saul's death. Chronicles seems to know of 1 Sam 28, and prps. of Sam 13:7–15a, but not of 1 Sam 15.

seek him/it in Saul's days" (13:3-4). The text alludes to 10:13-14; 12:24. David's diversion (*sbb*) of the ark complements Yhwh's diversion (*sbb*) of the kingship.

David's initial attempt to recover the ark (//2 Sam 6:1-11; in 1 Chron 13) fails. It does lead, however, first to his recognition by Hiram (14:1-2//2 Sam 5:11-12), and then to his victory over Philistia. In the first instance, David's kingship is "exalted upward" (*nś't lm‹lh*; 14:2). In the second, David receives what appears to be his first (and only) directly reported direct communication from god. These come in the form of war-oracles at David's request (14:10, 14; 2 Sam 5:19, 22-23). It seems that they imply some form of priestly intermediation. At any rate, the victory leads to the remark, "David's name went out among all the lands, and Yhwh instilled his fear in all the nations" (14:17).

The same sort of reciprocal Davidic behavior as that evinced in his first attempt to "divert the ark to us" marks the succeeding chapter. 1 Chron 14:1 reports that Hiram sent David workers to build him a house; 14:2 states that "David knew that Yhwh had established him firmly as king over Israel (*hkynw lmlk*), for his kingship was borne upward." 15:1 states, "He made himself a house/houses in the city of David, and established (*wykn*) a place for the ark of the deity, and pitched it a tent." The text continues with David's order that none but the Levites should "bear" (*nś'*) the ark. As Yhwh establishes, David establishes. As Yhwh bears upward, David prepares to bear upward.

1 Chron 15 begins with David's organization of the priestly and Levitic orders. Most revealing is v 13, which notes that Yhwh had aborted the earlier attempt at recovering the ark because "we did not seek him/it in the proper way." On this occasion, however, the bugs are ironed out; the ark comes without incident to the city. On this follows the eternal dynastic promise of 1 Chron 17 (2 Sam 7). The victories of 1 Chron 18 (2 Sam 8) ensue; these are punctuated by the signal remark: "Yhwh gave salvation to David wherever he went" (18:6, 13; 2 Sam 8:6, 14).

These chapters of Chronicles follow a distinctive pattern. The king seeks Yhwh; some recognition of his sovereignty ensues. He wins a victory. And, he prepares or organizes his followers. In David's case, the process is one of incremental rapprochement with Yhwh—the gradual closing of the rift created by Saul. At the same time, Yhwh glorifies David by increments: he is recognized first by Israel, then by Tyre, and finally, dynastically, by Yhwh. He conquers first Jerusalem, then the Philistines (at this point remedying the problem attacked by Saul), and finally all of Cis-Euphratia (esp. 18:3). He begins in 11:9 on the wax (*hālôk wᵊgādôl*), with Yhwh with him; in 14:7, his reputation extends across "all the lands," while "Yhwh instills his fear in all the nations"; and in 18:6, 13 comes the remark that Yhwh gave him *victory* everywhere, wherever he went. The progression is one of constant growth, of continual expansion. It is correlated to the progressive narrowing of the gap between Israel and her god.

Nevertheless, Chronicles is careful to reserve the final act of rapprochement. 1 Chron 16:39-42 report that Zadoq, Heman, and Jeduthun were stationed not at the ark in Jerusalem but at the tabernacle, domiciled at Gibeon. This particular is retrieved in 1 Chron 21:29-30. Though David has seen the angel of Yhwh (21:16), though Yhwh answers David with a sign (21:26), though David has acquired the future site of the temple (22:1), nevertheless, "David could not approach (the tabernacle of Yhwh) to seek god, for he was terrified by the sword of Yhwh's angel" (21:30). Here, one recalls the cherub stationed outside Eden. The tabernacle is the locus for communion with god. Chronicles recalls (21:29) that it is the tabernacle made by Moses—the model for Israel's communication with the deity (as Deut 34:10).

It is Solomon, thus, who bridges the last gap between Israel and Yhwh. At the very outset of his reign, Solomon sacrifices with all Israel at what Chronicles calls *ʾōhel môʿēd hā-ʾĕlōhîm* (2 Chron 1:3)—implying, perhaps, participation there in god's "meeting" or "appointed time." Correspondingly, Solomon receives what is probably the first direct communication from Yhwh to a king in Chronicles, and what is certainly the first unsolicited direct communication. Even more, despite the insistence of Kings that the appearance was a dream (1 Kgs 3:5, 15; but cf. 11:9), Chronicles states that Solomon received an epiphany (2 Chron 1:7). Solomon (who has yet another epiphany in 2 Chron 7:12-22 after the reunification in the temple of the ark and tabernacle—2 Chron 5:4-9; 1 Kgs 8:3-9—foreshadowed in 2 Chron 1:4) is the only king to attain this height. He is the king who achieves Israel's fullest reconciliation with Yhwh.

In connection with the Davido-Solomonic materials, it is the modality of reward employed by Chronicles that is of interest. The plainest is victory at war. This applies not only to David but also to Abijah (2 Chron 13:13-18—here *hēsēb* marks Jeroboam's failure where David in 1 Chron 14:14ff. is a success), Asa (14:6, 10-14), Jehoshaphat (20; esp. vv 27, 29, where god's fear falls on all the kingdoms of the lands, as in David's case), Amaziah (25:7-10, 11-13), Uzziah (26:5-7), Jotham (27:5-6), and Hezekiah (32:1-23), all of whom are said to have sought Yhwh in one form or another in the immediate context of their victories.

Nevertheless, other, equally important types of reward are associated with this one. Territorial expansion—particularly under David—is of some importance. Japhet has argued that from the time of the division Chronicles reports progressive Judahite conquest of the north. While her case has been refuted by Williamson,[4] her underlying perception remains valid: Chronicles evinces a strong interest in Israel's and Judah's territorial growth. Growth is one of the marks of divine favor.

In the same vein, Chronicles concerns itself with what it repeatedly calls "wealth and honor." David reduces Moab to vassalage—to bearers of tribute (1 Chron 18:2). He captures hordes of men and equipment from Hadadezer (18:4), and exacts tribute of Damascus (18:6). He despoils Aramea and Edom of gold and silver in apparently unlimited quantity (18:7-11), dedicating it to Yhwh. His regnal account closes with the remark, "[David ben-Yishai] died at a ripe old age, full of days, wealth and honor . . . " (1 Chron 29:28). The same concerns appear in the account of David's transferring the kingship to Solomon. 1 Chron 22 repeatedly stresses the infinity of wealth accumulated by David for the temple-building (vv 3-4, 5b, 14, 15, 16). The motifs surface yet again in 1 Chron 28-29, at the actual passing of the mantle (28:1, 14-18; 29:2-5, 6-8, 12, 21).

It is hardly necessary to dwell on the emphasis placed on Solomon's wealth in 2 Chron 1-9. Already at 2 Chron 1:12 he is promised wisdom, honor, and wealth exceeding that of any king before or after. The succeeding materials hasten to bear out the point (1:14-17; 2:6-9; 3:4-7, 14; 4:7-8, 18, 19-22; 5:1; 8:17-18). They culminate in the

---

4. See Williamson, *Israel*, pp. 100-101. The text so belies Japhet's scheme here that one suspects her of an understandable but unfortunate infatuation with the scheme.

remarks of 9:9-28, which include such statements as "silver was not reckoned as anything in Solomon's days" (9:20c) and "All the kings of Arabia [? the west], and the governors of the earth used to bring gold and silver to Solomon" (9:14b).

Nor is Solomon the only king rewarded with wealth or territory. Abijah seizes cities from Jeroboam (2 Chron 13:19). Asa carries off "very much spoil indeed" (14:12) from his encounter with Zerah (note 14:13-14). His *disbursal* of funds to Aram, by contrast, leads to his condemnation to war for the rest of his reign: The spoil of Aram eludes him; he dies of a hideous disease (16:7-13). Jehoshaphat, conversely, seeks Yhwh throughout his reign. He is rewarded with tribute from all Judah: "he had wealth and honor in quantity" (17:5; 18:1). The Philistines and Arabs pay him tribute (17:11), and, as in David's time, Yhwh's fear goes forth upon all the lands about (17:9; 20:29). Jehoshaphat waxes ever greater (*hôlēk wᵊgādēl ʿad lᵊmāʿlâ*)—again like David. His building activity burgeons (17:12b-19). His despoliation of Ammon, Moab, and Edom is so extensive as to require three full days (20:25).

By the same token, the early part of Joash's reign sees extensive royal capital accumulation (2 Chron 24:5-14). Only when Joash forsakes Yhwh is he, like his wicked predecessors Rehoboam (2 Chron 12:9) and Jehoram (21:16-17), plundered. Again, Amaziah despoils Edom while relying on Yhwh (25:9-10, 13). He in turn is despoiled (25:22-24) when and only when he rejects the divine counsel (25:14-16). Uzziah accumulates tremendous wealth and builds frantically, meanwhile extracting tribute from Philistia, Arabia, and Ammon (26:6-15), all because "He used to seek God in the days of Zechariah, who was understanding in fearing [or: seeing] God, and in the days of his seeking Yhwh, the deity gave him success" (26:5). Similarly, Jotham, who "established his ways before Yhwh his god" (27:6), built, conquered Ammon, and exacted tribute (27:3-5).

The unregenerate Ahaz is first pillaged (28:8), and then disappointed at the results of his disbursing funds (28:21), all because he did not seek Yhwh. He is deprived of his cities (28:17-19); he is generally despoiled (28:5ff.). But Hezekiah's reform reverses the situation. He reigns in opulence (30:24ff.; 31:4-12); he builds and creates (32:3-5). And, at his rescue, the text records, "Many brought tribute to Yhwh, to Jerusalem, and gifts to Hezekiah, king of Judah, and he was exalted in the sight of all the nations thereafter" (32:23). His regnal summary recalls David and Solomon in this regard (32:27-30).

Though these motifs disappear after the account of Hezekiah's reign, Chronicles up to that point is permeated with the notion that more is better. Wealth is good. Expansion is good. Growth is good (hence Solomon's exaltation—1 Chron 29:25, 2 Chron 1:1; esp. 2 Chron 9:22—Solomon was "greater" than all the kings of the earth with regard to wealth and wisdom—after David's, and before Jehoshaphat's and Hezekiah's—1 Chron 11:9; 17:6, 12; cf. 26:15-16; 2 Chron 32:23). Size is good—for example, the temple must be "big," Solomon says, "because our god is bigger than any god. And who could be strong enough to build him a house when the heavens—even the highest heavens—cannot contain him?" (2 Chron 2:4-5). Such emphases recur throughout—in Solomon's magnification at accession (1 Chron 29:25) so that he, "a youth and weak" (1 Chron 22:5; 29:1), will be capable of building the temple;[5] at the failure of the altar at

---

5. See my *Constitution*. I have argued there that this is a ritual actualized in narrative.

the temple dedication to contain all the sacrifices (2 Chron 7:7); at the inability of the priests to enter the new temple because it was so full of Yhwh's glory (2 Chron 6:14; 7:2–3).

Simply, from David through Hezekiah, Chronicles regards and bestows abundance as a mark of divine favor. This is illustrated by the distribution of the root *rbh*, "much, many." The vocable occurs 100 times in Chronicles, 96 times with positive or neutral force. Of the four occurrences with negative connotations, one—1 Chron 21:15—uses it in the sense "Enough!", to stop the slaughter of Israel by Yhwh's angel (and this is shared with 2 Sam 24:16). And two occur after Hezekiah's regnal report (2 Chron 33:6; 36:14; the fourth is 2 Chron 28:13). These are the only two instances of the root after Hezekiah. By contrast, Kings uses the root only 30 times, of which fully two-thirds occur in the account of Solomon's reign (as opposed to less than twenty percent in that account in Chronicles). Of the remaining 10 instances, at least 6, and possibly 8, carry negative connotations.

This difference, in fact, symptomizes the differences between Chronicles and Kings. Except in shared passages, after Solomon's reign, Kings virtually never speaks of Yhwh's rewarding a pious monarch with wealth. The very lexeme "wealth" (*ʿōšer*), which occurs eight times in Chronicles (1 Chron 29:12, 28: 2 Chron 1:11, 12; 9:22; 17:5; 18:1; 32:27), seven times in conjunction with "honor" (not in 2 Chron 9:22), occurs only three times in Kings (1 Kgs 3:11, 13; 10:23), all with regard to Solomon, and all with parallels in Chronicles (2 Chron 1:11, 12; 9:22). Kings is simply not oriented toward accumulation.

Within Chronicles, the motifs of nearness to god, of salvation, and of expansion, growth, and accumulation all merge into a single complex, characterized by the rest motif. The motif surfaces already in 1 Chron 22:9, where David recounts that Yhwh promised him a son:

> He will be a man of rest, and I shall give him rest from all his enemies from about. For Solomon (*šᵊlômô*) will be his name (*šᵊmô*), and well-being (*šālôm*) and quiet (*šeqeṭ*) I shall bestow on Israel in his days.

The motif resurfaces in 22:18, and especially in 28:3, in which David explains that he was prevented from building the temple because he was "a man of wars" (and 22:8). Moreover, 1 Chron 23:25 correlates Israel's rest with Yhwh's (23:26): because Yhwh has given rest to his people "from about," Israel is obliged to give rest to Yhwh; Solomon must build him a permanent dwelling. This same notion emerges in 1 Chron 28:2, where David calls the temple a "house of rest," a reference to Solomon, "a man of rest" (22:9). At the dedication of the temple, 2 Chron 6:41 retrieves the thought once again: Yhwh is called on to occupy his resting-place. The temple project is Solomon's reciprocation for the rest bestowed on Israel by Yhwh.

After Solomon, the theme continues to unfold. Though Abijah inherits the unrest caused by Jeroboam, Asa's reign represents a period of peace and quiet (2 Chron 13:23c; 14:4c, 5b, 6d; 15:15, 19), characterized by prosperity, expansion, and salvation at war, so long as his heart was "wholly with Yhwh." It is precisely at the point at which he abandons Yhwh that he is condemned to war for the remainder of his reign (16:9). Similarly, Jehoshaphat's reign is marked not just by union with Yhwh, or wealth, and so forth, but also by peace (17:10). As in Solomon's and Asa's cases, Jehoshaphat achieves "rest from about" (20:30). His is an era of quiet (20:30). And at Joash's accession, the text reads, "All the people of the land rejoiced and the city was quiet (*wat-tišqōṭ*). Athaliah they killed by the sword" (23:31). This is the response to Jehoiada's righteous acts.

This theme is consistently tied up with seeking Yhwh, with salvation, with prosperity, and so forth. Its final articulation comes in 2 Chron 32:22, toward the end of the Hezekiah account:

> Yhwh saved (*wš*ʿ) Hezekiah and the inhabitants of Jerusalem from the hand of Sennacherib king of Assyria and from everyone's hand, and he guided them from about (*wa-yᵊnahᵃlēm mis-sābîb*).[6]

Notices of tribute borne to Hezekiah, of Hezekiah's exaltation and wealth, of his humiliation before Yhwh all follow. This is the last occurrence of the term *mis-sābîb*, "from about," in Chronicles, and of the root *wš*ʿ, "save." The verse appears to form an inclusio of Hezekiah with David, who also was saved wherever he went (1 Chron 18:6, 13). From Manasseh onward, the whole rest/prosperity/salvation complex disappears.

The rest motif in Chronicles resembles closely that in Joshua and Judges (esp. 2 Chron 13:23; 24:4, 5; 20:30, 23:31 with Josh 11:23; 14:15; Judg 3:11, 30; 5:31; 8:28). Kings, however, evinces no such interest. It is noteworthy, for example, that the term *nṣl*, "rescue," occurs twelve times with regard to Hezekiah in Kings (nine of these shared with the Isaiah tradition in Isa 36–39, and three more in the same pericope), and only once elsewhere, in close proximity (2 Kgs 17:39). The root *yš*ʿ, "save," occurs in Kings seven times with reference to Israel, not Judah, twice in the Isaiah tradition material (2 Kgs 19:19, 34 = Isa 37:20, 35), and once with reference to Ahaz's importuning Tiglath Pileser (2 Kgs 16:7). The notion of Yhwh's intervention on behalf of the pious monarch is not explicitly elaborated.

The situation with the rest motif proper is even starker. Numerous commentators have taken 2 Kgs 11:20—"the people of the land rejoiced and the city was quiet"—to imply that syncretistic Jerusalem went into mourning at Athaliah's death.[7] In the context of Kings, where the lexeme *šqṭ* does not again appear, this interpretation is almost plausible. But Chronicles provides a context against which this verse demands to be read: the statement is unequivocally positive. The city was quiet—it was at rest.

The case of 2 Kgs 11:20 is in and of itself somewhat suspicious. Only at one other locus does the rest motif crop up in Kings—that is, in 1 Kgs 5:4, 18, in the account of Solomon's reign.[8] The latter is of greatest interest here.[9] In it, Solomon writes to Hiram:

---

6. For the vb., cf. Exod 15:13; note Pss 31:4; 23:2 for conjunction with *nwh*.

7. See, recently, J. Gray, *I & II Kings*, OTL, 2nd ed. (Philadelphia, 1970), p. 582.

8. I discount 2 Kgs 22:20; 2 Chron 34:28, in which Josiah is promised death "in peace, well-being (*bᵊšālôm*)," first, because the rest is not general; but second, even allowing that the context may imply that the phrase merely asserts that Josiah will not see Jerusalem's destruction, an interpretation which seems to me to founder on other uses of *šālôm* and the Israelite distinction between violent and natural death, the character of the rest is sufficiently fleeting to distinguish it from other instances in the histories. Otherwise—and far more probably—Josiah's Armageddon completely belies the promise, a fact with which Chronicles, at least, attempts to come to terms (2 Chron 35:21–22). 2 Kgs 20:19, from the Isaiah-tradition (Isa 39:8), is an intermediate instance.

9. On the former, cf. OG, and esp. 2:46f–g.

> You knew David my father, that he was not able to build a house to Yhwh's, his god's name, on account of the war that was about him, until Yhwh should give them over under the soles of his feet. So now, Yhwh my god has given rest to me from about; there is no opponent; there is none who does damage.

This sounds more like Chronicles than it does like Kings. David was prevented by his preoccupation with war from erecting a house to Yhwh. At least, like 1 Chron 22:9 with regard to 1 Chron 17, it stands in tension with the repudiation of the temple in 2 Sam 7. Certainly, it stands in tension with the remark of 2 Sam 7:1 that Yhwh had granted David "rest from about," though this is probably a late insertion. It *is* a remark ungrounded elsewhere in the former prophets, but it falls into quite a natural context if read in conjunction with Chronicles.

In this respect, 1 Kgs 5:4, 18; 2 Kgs 11:20 seem peculiar. Like the emphasis on wealth in Kings' account of Solomon's reign—like the stress of plenty, growth, and building there—the vestigial presence of the rest motif in three verses in Kings ought to evoke suspicion. In Chronicles, the whole account of Solomon's reign, which is quite similar to 1 Kgs 3–10, integrates nicely with the rest of the narrative up to the account of Hezekiah. Chronicles focuses consistently on rest, on quantity, on divine intervention. Kings is perversely sporadic in these regards. Thus, the term *lā-rōb* ("in quantity") occurs five times in Kings, all in the account of Solomon's reign, and two of them shared with Chronicles. Chronicles uses the same term fully thirty-five times, only seven times in reference to Solomon's reign, and last in 2 Chron 32:29—the end of the account of Hezekiah's reign. Again, Kings selects against the term *qhl* throughout. The root occurs nine times there, seven of them in 1 Kgs 8 (six shared with Chronicles) and two in 1 Kgs 12 (one shared with Chronicles). It is thus in relatively restricted usage.[10] Conversely, Chronicles uses the root frequently in connection with the Israelite assembly. It occurs thirty-eight times from David to Hezekiah, referring usually to the assembly constituted in either its sacral or its deliberative capacity.

There is little point in multiplying examples of this sort, except to indicate that they are both numerous and suggestive. The term *śmḥ* ("to rejoice"), for example, occurs only eight times in Kings. Of these, two are shared with Chronicles (1 Kgs 8:66; 2 Kgs 11:20 and 2 Chron 7:10; 23:21). A third derives from a shared passage (2 Kgs 11:14 from 11:20). And the remaining five (1 Kgs 1:40 *bis*, 45; 4:20; 5:21) are all concentrated in the first part of the account of Solomon's reign. In Chronicles, the root is distributed freely, occurring twenty-four times in all. Another example is that of the expression *heyôt ʿim lēb*. This occurs in 1 Kgs 10:2 (2 Chron 9:1); it also occurs in 1 Kgs 8:17–18 (2 Chron 6:7–8). The latter instance is of particular interest. In it, Solomon states that

---

10. J. Milgrom has kindly called my attention to his attempt to trace out a linear typology for the use of *qhl* and *ʿdh* in the Bible (*JQR* 1979, unavailable to me at the time of this writing). See also my treatment in my *Constitution.* I am a bit suspicious of the typological approach in vocabulary questions (less so in semantic, though I am still hesitant), since regional, personal, factional, and other preferences in selection necessarily intrude, and since the quantity of text on which we must base our typologies is so limited. In other words, the fact that P only of the Pentateuchal narrators uses the word *ʿēdâ*, "(sacred) community, (sacred) assembly" in no way suggests that the lexeme was unknown at the time when J wrote. The possibility is there; but the evidence is insufficient to prove it. At any rate, for the best attempt to impose chronological order on the biblical chaos, see R. Polzin, *Late Biblical Hebrew: Toward an Historical Typology of Biblical Hebrew Prose*, *HSM* 12 (Missoula, 1976).

David "had it in mind" to build a house for Yhwh, but Yhwh responded negatively. Chronicles, in which the same expression occurs eight times, grounds the remark fully. David himself has said as much in 1 Chron 22:7; 28:2. 2 Chron 1:11 has Yhwh respond (not in 1 Kgs 3:11) to Solomon, as to David in 1 Kgs 8:18//2 Chron 6:8, "Because you 'had it in mind,' I shall reward you in such-and-such a way." Indeed, after the account of Solomon's reign, Chronicles twice more uses the expression in connection with establishing a relationship with the deity (2 Chron 24:4; 29:10). There are no other instances in Kings.

Data of this nature, plentiful throughout the histories,[11] suggest two distinct possibilities. Either Chronicles seizes upon certain isolated, anomalous texts in Kings, and applies the values they reflect to reports concerning kings from David to Hezekiah,[12] or Chronicles draws consistently from a source used by Kings perhaps relatively heavily for the account of Solomon's reign,[13] but thereafter only irregularly. Of these possibilities, the former seems inherently unlikely.[14] The latter, that both histories draw on a common source, is naturally a possibility.

II

It is, fortunately, possible to shed some light on this subject by brief examination of the attitudes struck by Kings and Chronicles toward Davidic dynasty over Israel. On this point, the histories diverge widely.

Apart from the dynastic promise of 1 Chron 17, which duplicates that of 2 Sam 7 with minor variation,[15] Chronicles, like Kings, articulates Solomon's arrangement with Yhwh in conditional contractual terms. David prays that Yhwh will endow Solomon with the *śkl wbynh*, "sense and insight," that will enable him to "succeed" (1 Chron 22:11–13). He urges Solomon to "serve God" (28:9); he urges God to give Solomon a "whole mind, to observe" Yhwh's will (29:19). The issue, especially in 1 Chron 22:11ff., is whether Solomon will prove himself worthy of the dynastic award by observing Yhwh's statutes sufficiently to be allowed to complete the temple. In this regard, it appears that Chronicles does not take the remark in Samuel, "He will build me a house" (2 Sam 7:13; 1 Chron 17:12), as a lapidary prophecy. Rather, it serves for Chronicles as

11. I shall marshal a series of such cases in a volume, now in preparation, on the common source of Kings and Chronicles.

12. One might argue chronistic generalization of materials in Solomon's reign. However, such passages as 2 Kgs 11:20 (and, indeed, 2 Kgs 11 as a whole) and the anomalous character of those materials in Kings contraindicate that hypothesis. One must also strain somewhat to explain the absence of such values in Chronicles after Hezekiah. On the whole, the data are best organized by hypothesizing an earlier source.

13. See J. Liver, "The Book of the Acts of Solomon," *Bib* 48 (1967) 75–101, on the source cited in 1 Kgs 11:41. *Pace* Liver, the source is probably closer to 1 Kgs 3–10//2 Chron 1–9 than to anything else.

14. Professor N. Sarna notes (in conversation) the absence of music from Solomon's, but its prominence in Hezekiah's, temple ceremonies. This suggests neither pro- nor retrojection, but plain recording. See below, and my forthcoming study.

15. Specifically, Solomon, rather than David, is the recipient of the dynastic award. This may be the more authentic tradition (!). See F. M. Cross, *Canaanite Myth and Hebrew Epic* (Cambridge, Massachusetts, 1973), pp. 219–273. Cf. also the fine study of N. Sarna, "Psalm 89: A Study in Inner Biblical Exegesis" in *Biblical and Other Studies*, ed. A. Altmann, *Philip W. Lown Institute of Advanced Judaic Studies, Brandeis University. Studies and Texts*, 1 (Cambridge, Massachusetts, 1963), pp. 29–46.

an implicit protasis to the establishment of Solomon's dynasty forever. If Solomon is pious, he will complete the temple. If, in David's words, he "succeeds" in building the temple, Yhwh's promise will have come true.

For the account of Solomon's reign, this interpretation has important ramifications. There, and thereafter, two types of rehearsal of David's and Solomon's contracts are in evidence. Kings features one refrain that has no counterpart in Chronicles. This is the expression "for the sake of my servant, David," etc. (1 Kgs 11:34; 11:12, 13, 32; cf. 2 Kgs 20:6). Its alloforms invoke "the sake of my servant, David" to whom Yhwh promised a fief (*nîr*)[16] forever (1 Kgs 11:36; 15:4; 2 Kgs 8:19; 2 Chron 21:7).[17] This refrain accounts for ongoing Davidic ascendance in Judah and Jerusalem. It conveys the doctrine that under no circumstances will Yhwh revoke the Davidic charter there. What it amounts to, as Weinfeld and others have observed, is the justification for a land grant to the house of David.[18]

A second doctrine—that David's dynasty depends on his successors' behavior—is expressed with the clause, "There will not fail you/David a man sitting on the throne of Israel." This surfaces three times in Kings and twice in Chronicles (1 Kgs 2:2–4 [in the structural locus of 1 Chron 22:7–13 and with the shared term *škl*]; 8:25 [2 Chron 6:16]; 9:4–5 [2 Chron 7:17]; and cf. 2 Kgs 10:32; 15:12). A third text in Chronicles, 1 Chron 28:6–7, shares with them the notion that Solomon's dynasty hinged on his behavior as king.[19] However, as R. E. Friedman has observed, the texts that place the responsibility for the continuation of David's dynasty on Solomon's shoulders deal not with dynasty over a fief but with kingship over Israel.[20] That is, none of the fief-refrains deals specifically either with kingship or with any of its Hebrew metonyms: none mentions "Israel." None of the conditional ("there will not fail you . . . ") refrains addresses anything *but* kingship, and that always over Israel.

Unlike the fief-formulae, which are scattered throughout Kings, the refrain, "There will not fail you a man sitting on the throne of Israel—*if* you obey Yhwh's ordinances," along with all articulations of a conditional dynastic agreement with Solomon, are confined in Kings and Chronicles to the account of Solomon's reign. This intimates to what extent that reign served historiographically as a testing-ground for the dynasty. Chronicles emerges with an undeniably positive portrait of Solomon; Kings arrives at a negative evaluation. It is in the dynamic of their relationship in this regard that a clearer understanding of the histories can emerge.

Chronicles' view of Solomon is evinced in a variety of ways. For one thing, David states that only if Yhwh gives Solomon *škl wbynh*, "sense and insight," will Solomon "succeed" (1 Chron 22:12). At Gibeon, Solomon requests and receives *ḥkmh wmdᶜ*,

16. See Rashi on 1 Kgs 11:36; P. D. Hanson, "The Song of Heshbon and David's *Nîr*," *HTR* 61 (1968) 297–320.

17. The instance in 2 Chron 21:7 is drawn, with the surrounding vv, from 2 Kgs 8:17–22.

18. See M. Weinfeld, "The Covenant of Grant in the Old Testament and in the Ancient Near East," *JAOS* 90 (1970) 184–203; *Deuteronomy and the Deuteronomic School* (Oxford, 1972), pp. 74–81; Cross, *Canaanite Myth*, pp. 237–265; J. D. Levenson, "On the Promise to the Rechabites," *CBQ* 38 (1976) 508–514.

19. 1 Kgs 6:11–13, though related, is absent from OG and marked off as secondary by the epanalepsis 6:9a, 14. Read *brevior*. On epanalepsis, see S. Talmon, "The Presentation of Synchroneity and Simultaneity in Biblical Narratives," *Scripta Hierosolymitana* 27 (1978) 9–26.

20. See his *The Exile and Biblical Narrative* (Harvard Semitic Monographs 22, Chico, California, 1981). I have developed his insight in its historical connections in my *Constitution*.

"wisdom and knowledge" (2 Chron 1:7–13), not the same thing at all. But a letter from Hiram settles the issue decisively. Hiram starts: "In Yhwh's love for his people did he make you king over them" (2 Chron 2:10). This forms an inclusio with Sheba's recognition of the same fact in 2 Chron 9:8. A second inclusio encompasses this first: the concluding notices of Solomon's reign (2 Chron 9) report how extensively Yhwh fulfilled the promises he made, at the start of the reign, in the Gibeonite incubation.

Hiram's continuation is more revealing. He states:

> Blessed is Yhwh god of Israel, who made heaven and earth, and who gave David the king a son, wise, and knowing sense of understanding (*ḥākām yôdēăᶜ śēkel û-bînâ*), who will build a house for Yhwh, and a house for his kingship [or: a dynasty for his kingship (!)]. (2:11)

Apart from the paronomasia on *bn*, "son," *bynh*, "insight," and *bnh*, "build," in evidence here and often in this section of Chronicles, Hiram's letter communicates subliminally to the reader. The gift bestowed by Yhwh at Gibeon, "wisdom and knowledge" (*ḥkmh wmdᶜ*) encompasses and surpasses the standard of wisdom necessary for Solomon to establish his dynasty (*śkl wbynh*), producing a king who is "wise, having knowledge of sense and insight." Solomon does not merely meet the standard for securing the dynasty. He surpasses it, just as he surpasses all kings in wealth and in wisdom.

Chronicles' handling of Solomon's reign in no way deviates from any of these intimations. The two epiphanies, the accumulation of wealth, the successful completion of the temple (esp. after 1 Chron 22:7–13) leave no doubt that Solomon has fulfilled all conditions laid upon him. Solomon has discharged his several obligations, earning perpetual dynastic sway over Israel. 2 Chron 7:11—"in everything that entered Solomon's mind to do with regard to the temple of Yhwh or to his own house [or: dynasty], he succeeded"— confirms the point. And the statements of 2 Chron 9:22ff. should leave no doubt.

Kings, however, takes an alternate view. Although it adulterates some of the pro-Solomonic materials of chaps. 3–10, it does preserve much of the material contained in Chronicles. Where it diverges is primarily in 1 Kgs 11; there, it accuses Solomon of nothing less than outright apostasy (1 Kgs 11:1–8, 10).

It is likely that by the time Kings was written, Solomon had already attained the sanctified status accorded him by Chronicles and most of subsequent Jewish tradition. Thus, only "in Solomon's old age" (1 Kgs 11:4a) did he deviate from the righteous paths. Nevertheless, Kings reports that Solomon's wives "perverted him," so that "his heart was not wholly with Yhwh his god, as David's heart had been," and so forth. He "built altars to Chemosh, . . . Molech," etc. (v 7; see v 8), despite the fact that Yhwh had appeared to him twice (11:9; here the dreams are suddenly epiphanies). Solomon's altars, of course, are destroyed by Josiah (2 Kgs 23:13–14), a hint that leads Weinfeld, along with Cross and Lohfink,[21] to trace these reports, and Kings' negative attitude toward Solomon generally, straight to the Josianic court. But these reports have headier implications still.

In Kings, all the considerations above—Solomon's supposed saintliness, David's

---

21. See Weinfeld, *Deuteronomy*, pp. 168–169; Cross, *Canaanite Myth*, pp. 274–289; N. Lohfink, "Die Bundesurkunde des Königs Josias," *Bib* 44 (1963) 261–288.

fealty, Solomon's senile apostasy—have combined to produce a peculiar historiographic view: though Solomon precipitated by his apostasy the division of the kingdom, Yhwh nevertheless preserved, first, the integrity of the kingdom during his lifetime, and, second, a fief forever in Jerusalem for the sake of his servant David. The result is that Yhwh is said to have harassed Solomon throughout his reign. In particular, he incited the Edomite Hadad and the Aramean Rezin to revolt (1 Kgs 11:14-25), though these notices do not easily square with Kings' notion of Solomon's early fidelity. This material, too, is at best incidental to the historian, amounting to minor proofs for his interpretation. The climax, so far as he is concerned, and the damning verification, is the division of the Davidic empire (11:9-13, 26-40; 12:1ff.).

It is at this juncture precisely that Kings begins to invoke the fief-formula. The fief in Jerusalem is a cup of consolation to the Davidides deprived of Israel. Yet Chronicles, though cognizant of the Solomonic schism, finds no room for the formula. The reason is, Chronicles does not recognize the legitimacy of the northern secession.

A number of texts confirm this view. The historian states it straight out in Abijah's battle-taunt of Jeroboam (2 Chron 13:4-7):

> Hear me, Jeroboam and all Israel! Oughtn't you know that Yhwh the god of Israel gave the kingdom to David over Israel forever, to him and to his sons by a salt treaty? And Jeroboam ben-Nebat, Solomon ben-David's servant, arose and rebelled against his liege? and there were gathered to him desperadoes,[22] sons of bitches, and they took their stand against Rehoboam ben-Solomon? and Rehoboam was a youth and weak-hearted [or: weak-minded], and didn't nerve himself in their presence?

The historian then vindicates Abijah by reporting Yhwh's intervention on his behalf (2 Chron 13:14-20).

By the same token, Chronicles addresses Hezekiah's efforts to return Israel to the Davidic fold with considerable sympathy (2 Chron 30:1-11). Hezekiah's reconciliation of parts of the north to the Jerusalem cult and the Davidic line produces the greatest and happiest assembly since the time of Solomon (30:13, 18-20, 23, 25-26)—that is, since before the schism. Perhaps most important, while both Kings and Chronicles report alliances between Judah and Israel, Chronicles in each case enters a prophecy against the league (2 Chron 19:1-3; 20:35-37; 25:7-9; prps. 21:6, 12ff.). And certainly most obviously, Chronicles averts its narrative eye from materials that concern the northern kingdom. This practice extends so far that there is no report of Jeroboam's making the golden calves, though Abijah alludes to them. There is no "sin of Jeroboam." There is no report of the north's fall. It is not that Chronicles is uninterested in the matter—as Abijah's speech makes clear. Nor is it indifferent to the northern population—Hezekiah's attempt at conciliation, among other texts (e.g., 2 Chron 28:5-15; 2 Chron 10:17; 31:1 on "all Israel in Judah" from Rehoboam to Hezekiah), is incompatible with

---

22. *ʾănāšîm rēqîm*. Dahood is in my view entirely correct in connecting the term with **ryq* (Heb. "unsheathe" in C. Dahood's "army, troops"). See his *Psalms* 1-3, *AB* 16, 17, 17a (Garden City, N.Y., 1965-1970), 1.7-8, 195, 210. However, like the English idiom "eat humble pie," which derives from the medieval English practice of feeding umbles pies to feudal retainers, the Hebrew expression has undergone a congeneric (and paronomastic semantic) assimilation, in this case with *rēq*, "empty," and taken on the connotation "worthless, shiftless, good-for-nothing." Cf. already EA 292:47; 297:14 for *rēq* (EA *ri-ki*) as "worthless, nothing to lose" (cf. 2 Kgs 4:3).

that hypothesis. The point is, Chronicles does not recognize the legitimacy of the division. It will not therefore report the course of northern history. Kings, which does recognize the schism, reports that history throughout. Each history justifies itself by appeal to Solomon's reign.

There are substantial indications that underlying the negative appraisal of Solomon in Kings is an originally pro-Solomonic source. Thus, every articulation of the dynastic covenant in Kings has a parallel or mirror text in Chronicles.[23] The structure of 1 Kgs 3-10 closely resembles that of 1 Chron 1-9. Much of the material is shared verbatim.

Second, the Kings dynastic promises, like those of Chronicles, appear in an atmosphere of general optimism. It is up to the reader to determine in the succeeding chapters whether Solomon has performed in the way specified by David (1 Kgs 2:2-4). However, it is plain from the ensuing verses that he managed to execute the blood-purge David enjoined on him at the same time (2:5-9 with vv 28-34, 36-46). Nor do the succeeding chapters intimate at any time that he deviated from the righteous way.

By the same token, Solomon's plea that Yhwh fulfill his promise to David—at the temple dedication (8:25-26; 2 Chron 6:16-17)—should evoke very positive expectations. Cases are rare in HB of characters making positive requests of Yhwh to no avail.[24] There is none of which I am aware in which a character as guiltless as Solomon is at this point in Kings (or throughout in Chronicles) is rebuffed or disappointed by God.[25] It may be noted, too, that Solomon's request is couched in a phrase, *yēʾāmēn dᵊbārkā* (8:26; 2 Chron 6:17), which, used elsewhere by Chronicles (1 Chron 17:23-24; 2 Chron 1:9) but not by Dtr, appears to connote an abiding fulfillment (2 Chron 1:9). If so, the mitigation of the conditionality of the dynastic promise is implied.

1 Kgs 9:2-5, the last articulation of the dynastic agreement in Kings (2 Chron 7:17-18), presents yet another interesting point. The text affirms that the conditional agreement remains in force. It promises perpetual enfranchisement to Solomon's line over Israel. 9:6-9, probably but not certainly an Exilic insertion, confront Israel with the possibility of exile (2 Chron 7:20-22). That is, the text provides for the Israelites' destruction; it holds out nothing but promise for the Davidides.

To á limited extent, even the Gibeonite incubation seems to share this understanding (1 Kgs 3:5-15). The text states that Yhwh is fulfilling his dynastic obligations to David (v 6). The test erected by the text—the potential reward for Solomon's fidelity—is length of reign (3:14). This is the issue that Solomon's behavior will decide. First, the implication seems to be a tacit understanding concerning the ongoing nature of the dynasty. Second, the fact that Solomon reigned for forty years must imply at least a modicum of fidelity on his part.

Apart from such hints, and *mutatis mutandis* in conjunction with them, the presence of an occasional editorial apostil to the effect that Solomon fulfilled his obligations to

---

23. On the exception, 1 Kgs 6:11-13, see above, n. 19.

24. Jonah (Jon 4:3, 8-9) and Elijah (1 Kgs 19:4) ask to die, and receive lessons in meteorology instead. The case of Job is a bit more intricate and is arguable from either position.

25. David's prayer for his sick love-child is rebuffed (2 Sam 12:15-20). But this is a specific punishment for a (specific) sin (12:14). Generally, biblical narrators are not interested in the prayers of the kinds of characters whose prayers would be rebuffed. This is quite plainly the case in the Pentateuch, the Former Prophets, and Chronicles.

the deity is decisive. 1 Kgs 3:3, for example, states that "Solomon loved Yhwh, adhering to the statutes of David his father. . . . " The Gibeonite episode concludes, "Divine wisdom was in him to perform justice" (3:28). Subsequent texts insist on his wisdom and demeanor (5:9-14, 26; 10:3-4, 9, 23-24), on the peace and prosperity he enjoyed (4:20; 5:1, 4-26; 10:1-29, etc.), and so forth. The atmosphere implies a positive evaluation of his performance.

Given this information, and given especially the integration of the material on Solomon's reign shared in 2 Chron 1-9 and 1 Kgs 3-10 with the rest of Chronicles, it is difficult to resist staking a conclusion: there was a source common to Chronicles and Kings, on which Chronicles relied more consistently than did Kings. This source seems to have been favorable to Solomon. It seems to have affirmed eternal Davidic dynasty over the northern tribes. It seems to have exuded the optimism of an expansive community.[26]

III

If one were to seek a source underlying Kings and Chronicles, the logical period to which to assign it would be that of Hezekiah. There are several hints in the opening genealogies that this is the case. One speaks of the enrollment of a genealogy in Hezekiah's time (1 Chron 4:41). The Saulide lists have eleven and thirteen generations in them (1 Chron 8; 9). Curiously, there are thirteen generations from David to Hezekiah. Moreover, the last instance of the term "enroll," (*htyḥś*) in Chronicles, used with reference to the genealogies, is found precisely in the account of Hezekiah's reign (2 Chron 31:16, 17, 19).

But sounder indications are to be sought in the formulaic variation after Hezekiah.[27] Every accession formula in Kings (barring Asa's, Jehoram's, and Ahaz's) for the kings of Judah reports the name of the queen mother. This continues down to the Exile. In Chronicles, however, the queen mother's name disappears after Hezekiah, though it is consistently present to that point. This does not, on the surface of things, seem likely to be a literary device.

Similarly, the burial notices both of Kings and of Chronicles undergo a significant shift after Hezekiah's. In Chronicles, most of the notices up to that point stipulate burial "in the city of David" (*bʿyr dwd*). None of those after Hezekiah does (2 Chron 33:20, 24; 35:24). Here, a similar phenomenon is present in Kings: up to Hezekiah, all kings are buried "in the city of David." Thereafter, none is (2 Kgs 21:18, 26; 23:30). There is a palpable break at Hezekiah's time.

There are other indications in Kings that some Hezekian source was in use by the "Deuteronomist." For example, 2 Kgs 18:5 states that Hezekiah was greater than any king who came after or before him. 2 Kgs 23:25 makes a remarkably similar statement about Josiah. Moreover, while Chronicles reports prophetic activity throughout Judah's history, Hezekiah is the first king in Judah, according to Kings, to confront a prophet

26. See above, n. 12. Since 1 Kgs 3-10 derive from a source in any case, and since that source is probably the one from which 2 Kgs 11 is drawn (and note the convergence with Chronicles there), its concern with the temple should probably be mooted.

27. See H. Macy, "The Sources of the Books of Chronicles: A Reassessment" (diss. Harvard, 1975), for the raw data.

since the Solomonic schism. There is, in each account, something periodic about Hezekiah's reign. Hezekiah, for Kings, is the first king to remove the high places. In both histories, he is the last king of Israel or Judah of whom it is explicitly stated that God was with him (2 Kgs 18:7; 2 Chron 32:7-8). In Chronicles, God is last with Necho, and against Josiah (2 Chron 35:21). It is perhaps to be inferred that he is also later with Cyrus (2 Chron 36:22-23).

Within Chronicles, other schemes are in evidence. A relatively weak example is that of the notion of "strength, consolidation." The clearest usage here is that of 2 Chron 1:1: "Solomon ben-David, 'took hold' over his kingship" (*way-yithazzēq ʿal malkûtô*). This stands where one would expect the accession formula to appear. It is associated with Yhwh's aid, and it leads immediately to the establishment of communication at the tabernacle. Similar statements are made about Rehoboam (2 Chron 12:13a; note esp. 13:7; contrast 11:7 and then 12:1), David (1 Chron 11:10), Abijah (2 Chron 13:21), Jehoshaphat (2 Chron 17:1), Jehoram (2 Chron 21:4), and Jehoiada (2 Chron 23:1), who was buried in the graves of the kings (2 Chron 24:16), though his protégé, Joash, was not (2 Chron 24:25).[28] In these cases, the term relates either to taking hold of the kingship or to the accession formulae of the king.

In other cases, the reference, and even occasionally the *binyan* of the verb, is different. Thus, Asa "takes hold" immediately before his reform (2 Chron 15:8; 16:9 is more difficult). Amaziah "takes hold" (2 Chron 25:11) by obeying Yhwh's orders just before leading troops into battle. The notice, "when the kingdom was firmly in his grip" (25:3—*kaʾăšer hāzᵊqâ ham-mamlākâ ʿālāyw*; the same phrase has crept into 2 Kgs 14:5, one of two applications of the root to the kingship in all of Kings), forms the preface to his regnal record. The root occurs in similar bearings with regard to Uzziah (26:5, 8, 15, 16—cf. 12:1), Jotham (27:6 with vv 7-9), and, finally, Hezekiah (32:5—in preparation for war with Assyria; Hezekiah, like Uzziah, is humbled in 32:25-26).

In all, Chronicles applies the verb *hzq*, often in the *hitpaʿel* (Dt), to every Judahite king from David to Hezekiah, with the exceptions of Ahaziah and Ahaz. The last occurrence of the *hitpaʿel* refers to Hezekiah. In each case, there is some more or less general connotation to the usage. Contrariwise, after Hezekiah, the root is nowhere applied in the same connections.[29] It would be too much to suggest a deliberate connection between the use of *hzq* in Chronicles and the name Hezekiah (*hzqyh*).[30] At the same time, the disturbance in this case after Hezekiah is nearly as stark as the disappearance of the queen mothers' names at that point. Perhaps it is even more significant.

In this context of the breakdown of formulae, the breakdown of various Chronistic motifs at Hezekiah elicits no surprise. Hezekiah is the last king of whom it is reported that Yhwh was with him, saved him, rescued him, gave him any sort of rest, brought foreigners to pay tribute to him, and so forth. This is peculiar: an author who reports as frequently as does Chronicles that Yhwh entreated will not rebuke, that Yhwh, once

---

28. Jehoiada is a royal figure for Chronicles. His 130-year life span is plain testimony to his righteousness; his burial among kings is proof.

29. It pops up in 2 Chron 34:8, 10; 35:2, in the first two occurrences with regard to reinforcing the temple, and in the third with regard to reinforcing the priestly orders. These are pedestrian usage, and far from the more formulaic usage of Chronicles up to Hezekiah.

30. In conversation, however, Professor S. Talmon has drawn my attention to Isa 39:1, which, especially in the context of the preceding verses (esp. 38:16-17, 19-21) with their plethora of *hets*, looks very much like intentional paronomasia.

sought, will not repudiate (1 Chron 28:9; 2 Chron 15:2; 28:11; 30:6, 8, 9; 14:6, etc.), is not the author to produce the story of Josiah's death. Chronicles will produce Amaziah's or Rehoboam's or Uzziah's or Asa's or Joash's backsliding, Manasseh's or Hezekiah's or David's regeneration. But it will not kill an innocent king, as it does Josiah. It will not—as it does in the case of Josiah—report Yhwh's championing an alien army. Josiah is the only Judahite king in Chronicles to die untimely, yet innocent of active trespass. He is the only king against whom Yhwh takes an active stance. He is the only king unreservedly endorsed by Chronicles whose accumulation of "wealth" is not reported. Even the simple formula "wealth and honor" disappears after Hezekiah.

Generally, there is no enumerating the thematic shifts at Hezekiah in Chronicles. The examples above can serve to create only an impressionistic effect. The text jettisons thereafter the entire rest-motif complex. The break is substantial. The break is clean.

At the same time, there is another path by which the break at Hezekiah in Chronicles can be established: there is an inclusio formed there between Hezekiah and the "United Monarchy." This has been recognized by various authors.[31] Williamson, for example, notes the emphases on Hezekiah's and Solomon's wealth (2 Chron 32:27-29; 9:13ff.), on the bringing of tribute to both (9:23-24; 32:23), on the two-week length of the festival of temple dedication (7:8-9; 30:23, 26), and so forth.[32] It would be difficult, additionally, to miss other bracketing devices—for example, Hezekiah's Passover is described as the height of joy since the time of Solomon (2 Chron 30:26). And the duties ascribed to the priests in Hezekiah's time (2 Chron 31:3) are precisely those described in the time of Solomon (1 Chron 16:39-40; 23:31; 2 Chron 2:3; 8:13; cf. Isa 1:13-14). The notion of the priests' self-sanctification occurs only in the accounts of Solomon's and Hezekiah's reigns (2 Chron 5:11; 29:15, 34). And other items of a lexical and a thematic nature fall into the same scheme.

There is very little point in multiplying examples here. It may be worth observing that with regard to Hezekiah and Solomon only (2 Chron 31:21; 7:11), Chronicles affirms that the king succeeded in all he sought to do with regard to the temple. It may be worth noting that Hezekiah (2 Chron 32:22), like David (1 Chron 18:6, 13), and, by implication, like Solomon, was successful in whatever he did. It may be worth observing that, like Solomon (2 Chron 1:1ff.), Hezekiah recovers access to the tabernacle (2 Chron 29:6—*way-yasseb penêhem*!), which Ahaz had shut off (2 Chron 28:24). It is important that unlike Rehoboam (2 Chron 12:14), but like the people under Solomon (1 Chron 22:19; 29:18), Hezekiah "fixed all his heart to seek Yhwh" (2 Chron 30:19, and cf. 28:8-9; cf. 19:3; 20:33). It is revealing that Yhwh listens to Hezekiah and cures the people of their impurity (2 Chron 30:20), the sort of tailored miracle that stands out in any biblical book.[33] And it seems impressive that of the first six Hezekian Levitic leaders enumerated (2 Chron 29:12), five have names identical with those in the genealogies of David's appointees to the temple service (1 Chron 6:20, 21, 29, 5-6, 6).

31. See, recently, R. J. Coggins, *1 & 2 Chronicles* (Cambridge, England, 1977), on Hezekiah.

32. See Williamson, *Israel*, pp. 120-125.

33. It may be that the historian understood the "miracle" in a less-than-miraculous sense. So, for example, Yhwh cleansing the people may mean nothing more than that priestly (prps. divinatory) dispensation was obtained. In very much the same way, Chronicles summarizes the civil war after Saul's death by the phrase "Yhwh diverted the kingdom to David ben-Jesse" (1 Chron 10:14). Scholars will need to pay more attention to the modes of Israelite discourse in future attempts to understand the text and reconstruct the history.

Nevertheless, the strongest evidence is the repetition in Hezekiah's account of themes first set out with regard to the United Monarchy. These have been reviewed above. The culmination of the rest-motif, with its associated notions of salvation, of prosperity, of abundance, of honor abroad, of foreigners bringing tribute—all in Hezekiah's reign—the fact that Hezekiah's Passover is specifically compared to Solomon's temple dedication (2 Chron 30:26), the fact that Hezekiah is the first king since Solomon to address all Israel "from Beersheba unto Dan" (2 Chron 30:5; 1 Chron 21:2 and 2 Chron 2:16)[34] all contribute to the general impression. That Hezekiah is said to have

> stationed the Levites at the house of Yhwh with timbrels, with lyres and with flutes, according to the command of David and Gad the royal seer and Nathan the prophet, because the command was from Yhwh's hand, from the hand of his prophets (29:25),

recalling thereby Solomon's receipt of the temple plans written by Yhwh's hand, from David, and his stationing of the Levites in the Davidically ordained order (2 Chron 5:12-13 with 1 Chron 28:11, 19), indicates a conscious correspondence.

Vestiges of the correspondence between Solomon and Hezekiah have even crept in Kings. Thus, David enjoins Solomon to piety,

> *lə-maʿan taśkîl bə-kōl ʾašer taʿaśeh*, in order that you may do wisely/fittingly in all that you do. (1 Kgs 2:3)

And 2 Kgs 18:7 reports of Hezekiah,

> *bə-kōl ʾăšer yēṣēʾ yaśkîl*, in everything he ventured he did wisely/fittingly.

These are the only such remarks in Kings. Chronicles regards Hezekiah as a second Solomon. The presence of the same motif in Kings, which is antagonistic to Solomon, suggests that the motif was a legacy of some prior, common source.

Though the sort of lexical evidence that might be adduced to support this construct does not lend itself to sufficiently compressed presentation for inclusion in this context, a last thematic observation is worth expressing. Both Kings and Chronicles tend to erect certain narrative tensions around which to construct the history. In Kings, these are overwhelmingly negative: the major ones are, when will Yhwh eradicate the north, and when will Yhwh eradicate Judah? When will Yhwh avenge the sin of Jeroboam, and when will Yhwh repay the wickedness of Judah's kings? Within these larger tensions, there are, of course, smaller ones. When will Yhwh eradicate the houses of Jeroboam, Baasha, and Omri? Will Yhwh fulfill his dynastic promise to Jehu, and when will he eradicate Jehu's house? Will Josiah destroy the Bethel sanctuary? Will Jezreel's dogs take their portion of Jezebel? In fact, of all the prophecy-fulfillment schemes selected by von Rad in Kings,[35] only three are potentially positive: the fulfillment of the promise to David that a son would sit on his throne (1 Kgs 8:20; 2 Chron 6:10); the four-generation promise of dynasty to Jehu (2 Kgs 10:30; 15:12);[36] and the prophecy that Josiah would

---

34. See Williamson, *Israel*, p. 123, on the interpretation of *ʾrṣ yśrʾl* in 2 Chron 2:16. His discussion typifies his strong grasp on the material.

35. See von Rad, *Studies in Deuteronomy*, SBT 9 (London, 1953), pp. 78-82. Von Rad has, of course, restricted himself artificially. Chronicles, too, contains the element of prophecy-fulfillment. This is only a single narrative device among many; its importance can quite easily be distorted. In fact, one might well call the prophecy itself a release from tension, since the fulfillment is by and large mechanical.

36. Von Rad does not list this case, probably because there is no notice of prophetic mediation. But 2 Kgs

not see the coming destruction of Jerusalem (2 Kgs 22:15ff.; 23:30). The first lies partially outside the book (von Rad cites the promise in 2 Sam 7:13) and derives from older materials (probably the common source) that had become traditional (cf. Pss 89; 132, *inter alia*). The second is merely dilatory of the eradication of Jehu's house (note 2 Kgs 10:31). And the third is similarly dilatory, but of an even greater disaster. Kings, that is to say, does not portray a world rife with milk and honey.

The narrative tensions in Chronicles stand in a marked contrast. There, the first question (after "Will these genealogies and lists ever end?") is, will David seek and find Yhwh? Will David recover communication with God? Will Solomon complete the rapprochement? Will Solomon earn perpetual dynasty? Will Hezekiah return Israel from limbo to the Davidic fold? Most of the tensions in Chronicles are quite positive in their narrative bearings. Chronicles asks, how will a problem be solved? How will Israel's lot ameliorate? Kings asks, conversely, when is the axe going to fall?

Yet, after the account of Hezekiah's reign, Chronicles ceases to ask the same sort of question. In fact, it seems to erect no narrative tensions at all. Events follow in sequence; but no expectations are evoked in the reader. The suggestion is, the work was geared to climax and to culminate in the account of Hezekiah's reign.

The foregoing argumentation has by necessity been impressionistic. It nevertheless opens up the possibility that a common source underlies Kings and Chronicles. This is not to say that Chronicles does not depend also on Kings—the statements that Asa and Jehoshaphat removed the *bāmôt*, for example, are juxtaposed with remarks taken from Kings that the *bāmôt* remained (2 Chron 14:2; 15:17; 17:6; 20:33). The fief-formula even occurs once in Chronicles (2 Chron 21:7), though it is wholly irrelevant to that work as it stands. But the vestigial presence in Kings of language and motifs full-blown in Chronicles strongly suggests common reliance on a prior source. The strong articulation of Hezekiah's correspondence to Solomon and the stark shift of interest after Hezekiah point directly to a source from Hezekiah's era.

That is, in much the same measure as Josiah's court produced a "Deuteronomistic" history, it seems that Hezekiah's court produced an extensive historical work of its own. This work, used sparingly in Kings, formed the broader base for Chronicles. Possibly, given the distribution of the rest motif in Joshua and Judges, it actually embraced what later became the "Deuteronomistic history." At all events, it exalted Solomon,[37] rejected northern independence, and looked forward to a period of expansion, of wealth, or of reconstitution. It viewed the destruction of the north with equanimity—as a chance

---

10:30 is open to the interpretation that the message came secondhand, or, rather, that the historian or his source understood that to be the case. 1 Sam 30:8 reports that Yhwh spoke to David; a glance at the preceding verse establishes that priestly mediation of the message is in point. It is perfectly plausible, thus, that 2 Kgs 10:30 represents a similar instance, but without the contextual control. Similarly, 2 Sam 5:19, 23-24; 1 Chron 14:10, 14-15 look very much like mediated war-oracles, though no notice of the mediation appears in the context.

37. Note further Prov 25:1. Hezekiah's dabbling with wisdom suggests further preoccupation with Solomon at his court. Thus, the intuition of R. B. Y. Scott that Hezekiah's court was the fount of Solomon's reputation, though ineptly argued, evinces a certain prescience. See his "Solomon and the Beginnings of Wisdom in Israel" in *Wisdom in Israel*, ed. M. Noth and D. W. Thomas, *VTSup* 3 (Leiden, 1955), pp. 262-279. More recently, see Weinfeld, *Deuteronomy*, pp. 161-162. Unfortunately, the notion that "wisdom"—the reification and restriction of which in the last quarter-century seem somewhat to have abated, yet without producing the rush to find "ignorance literature" and a "stupidity tradition" that one would expect in response— originated at Hezekiah's court seems to me to stem from the character and origins of the sources more than

for reunification of Israel with the Davidic line. It left its mark on all subsequent Israelite historiography.

IV

The present context does not afford space for extensive ramification on the basis of what precedes. These materials do suggest, however, a few points of general interest. First, the biblical historian—the redactor, arranger, tradent, whatever—was prepared to live with logical contradictions. This is true of Kings, of Chronicles, of Samuel, of Joshua, and of the Pentateuchal historians as well. The Israelite historian seems to have respect for his sources. Moreover, the apparent emphases of biblical compositions—of Chronicles on Davidic kingship, the unity of Israel, and on royal "consolidation, taking hold," of Kings on Solomon's positive achievements and on Hezekiah's piety—may be dictated in some measure by the use of sources. Chronicles ends with Yhwh championing two foreign kings, with Cyrus urging Judah to return and rebuild the temple under his authority. This is hardly a defense of Davido-Solomonic rule.

Second, it may be that the historiographic enterprise was one undertaken in monarchic Judah on a basis more extensive, and to a degree more sophisticated, than most of biblical scholarship is prepared to countenance. If Kings includes texts affirming (1 Kgs 4; 5:27–28, 29–32) and denying (1 Kgs 9:22)[38] Solomon's conscription of Israelites, if Chronicles includes texts affirming and denying Asa's and Jehoshaphat's removal of the *bāmôt*, one must reckon with the possibility not just that one or more historical traditions preceded but that historiography was sufficiently developed to deal with the problem, albeit in its own terms. Key, therefore, is the issue of selection. Thus, Kings selects less freely from the putatively Hezekian source than does Chronicles; Chronicles selects from Samuel only the materials pertinent to its enterprise.[39] But selection and criteria must be examined in some serious manner. On the flip side, there is nothing to say that Isaiah's account of Uzziah's reign (2 Chron 26:22) or, perhaps, of Hezekiah's (32:32) was not the equal of any other work in sophistication or breadth. Israel's historiographic tradition is as hoary as J, perhaps hoarier. To neglect that fact is, I think, a signal miscalculation.

Third, and finally, it seems likely that we are dealing here with a written document, a thematically integrated account. The evidence suggests to me that it encompasses all that we now call "Deuteronomistic history," from Joshua to Kings. I have no doubt that this suggestion, if noted, will be called into question, that the thesis of this presentation will be subject to attack. Still, whether it is right or wrong, it strikes me that accretional, redactional, and other models—the question *cui bono*? asked *a posteriori* will

---

from any semblance of historical reality. See below, p. 53. The fact that much of our documentation comes from the last century and a half of Judah's early independence hardly precludes the possibility of an extensive written literature from earlier times. Quite the reverse: the consolidation of literature, its assembly, its collection, in the seventh century suggests a literary legacy of considerable size.

38. See Gray, *Kings*, pp. 155–156, for the most reasonable of the many attempts to explain the contradiction away. It seems to me, however, that the tension remains strong.

39. Chronicles may not have had Samuel in its present form, of course. Or, if the Samuel materials were included already in the source used by Chronicles, the source may not have had the current text. Especially 2 Sam 11:2–12:25 looks very much like an insertion. Possibly it seems so because the historian is integrating two different sorts of records about David's reign.

not suffice to explain either the thematic generalization in Chronicles of materials anomalous in Kings—from the term *ḥṣṣrwt* in 2 Kgs 11:14, a "technical term" shared here with Chronicles, which uses it more than once, in a shared context, to broader themes, such as the rest motif—or the manifest ideological stratigraphy of both Chronicles and Kings. I therefore incline toward placing the supposed source in the reign of Hezekiah, the only king for whose reign literary activity is documented (Prov 25:1), and the king whose era produced the first prophetic books (that remain extant, of course).

At the same time, what with J and Judges and the so-called Court History, it behooves us to recognize the existence of a complex of literature antedating Hezekiah, and largely unknown to us. Chronicles, citing its sources, makes known the existence of a fair body of documents. This is no deception. We may find, underlying Kings, an extensive historical account. We are almost certain to find, underlying Kings, an extensive historiographic tradition. Before we ask, *"cui bono?"* we may profitably inquire, is this an isolated phenomenon? Is this a constant of pre-Exilic Israel? If so, the criteria for the inclusion of materials and the methods employed—if any—to rework, as well as to supplement, materials assume a prime interest.[40]

Israel's was an historically oriented culture, as even commonplace biblical scholarship will concede. In such a culture, historiography is no alien being. On the contrary, we may expect the records to be as extensive as they are for any ancient culture. Only, we must be open both to the possibility of their existence and to the subtlety of their influence. In David's "court history," Israel presents us with the most sophisticated historiography until Suetonius. She wines us on politics; she dines us on personality. That from the tenth century to the seventh she should impose an historiographic moratorium on herself is sufficiently improbable to command disbelief. In all likelihood, Israel had a flourishing historiographic tradition. Scholars may or may not be able to effect its recovery. But it is the duty of the historian to bear the possibility into account—in his reconstructions, in his researches, and in his deliberations. Treatments delinquent in this regard impoverish themselves, impoverishing the society that is their subject.

---

40. Unfortunately, this consideration calls for a reevaluation of the "common authorship" of Chronicles and Ezra-Nehemiah. Depending upon the use of sources, common authorship remains a possibility. Here, principles of selection, exclusion, and reworking have prime importance.

CASE STUDIES

Polemics and Apology in
Biblical Historiography—2 Kings 17:24-41
SHEMARYAHU TALMON

I

Scholars generally have concurred in the opinion that Chapter 17 in 2 Kings, which reports on the last days of the northern kingdom and the fate of the land after the capture by the Assyrians, should be viewed as a separate entity. Irrespective of its ascription to this or another author, redactor, or reviser, it is discussed as a self-contained unit. At the same time, it is the common view that Ch. 17 cannot be taken to be uniform, but, rather, is constituted of a variety of smaller components. The emerging picture poses a number of questions with regard to the identity of the authors of the diverse components, the identity and the aim of the various hands that had been at work in bringing about the present combination of texts and, in some cases, the wording of especially prominent verses and collocations. Some scholars apply to the analysis of the passage under review, as to the entire Book of Kings, the techniques of the sources theory perfected in the study of the Pentateuch. Others maintain that, being a work of historiography proper, this book requires different modes of approach which subsequently could possibly be applied to other biblical books, including the Pentateuch. The criticism leveled against the established sources-theory and a proposition for a novel approach were succinctly summarized by A. Jepsen in the introduction to his work *Die Quellen des Koenigsbuches*: "The sources-analysis of the Book of Kings was carried out for too long in the shadow of the critical analysis of the Pentateuch. . . . From this resulted that no generally accepted uniform solution of the problems was found with respect to either the Pentateuch or the other books. . . . Should therefore not an attempt be made to approach the sources analysis from an altogether different starting point . . . which might lead to clearer results?" However, in practice, Jepsen's attempt and the conclusions at which he arrived were not superior to those his predecessors had presented, and they did not settle the differences of opinion regarding the structure and composition of 2 Kings 17.

Editor's Note: The text of this chapter appears here in the form in which it was presented by the author at the University of California, San Diego, Conversation in Biblical Studies. For this reason, it does not include an apparatus of notes and references to previous publications.

It would seem that to some degree the divergencies resulted from a not sufficiently accurate definition of the textual unit and of the subunits to be investigated, and from the ongoing application of established stereotypes to their identification. What is more, not enough thought was given to the literary process by which the diverse components had been combined into their present form, i.e., to its *Tradierungsgeschichte*. And lastly, with some noteworthy exceptions, only peremptory attention was given to the historical circumstances and religious convictions which facilitated the emergence of the above textual unit in its present form, and which, to some degree, can yet be elicited from the text. To this task my presentation is directed. It will be based on a structural analysis, meant to define more succinctly the different literary pericopes which can yet be discerned in the present textual web, without having recourse to techniques which had evoked Jepsen's criticism. Once the major subunits have been defined, I shall try to trace the process of their incorporation into the larger framework, and, finally, to depict the means by which Ch. 17 as a whole was "inlibrated" into the Book of Kings. It is hoped that this investigation will permit us to define the circles which formulated the text in its present form and the reasons behind its infusion into the Book of Kings.

II

The overall extent of the composite unit under review can be fairly securely established with the help of the structural technique known as *Wiederaufnahme*. This technical device seemingly was employed by biblical authors and redactors (or arrangers) in the splicing of independent or semi-independent but nevertheless related narrative strands. It proffers to the reader what may be defined as an objective criterion for determining yet-discernible "joints" in the present fabric of the text. Being a technical scribal phenomenon, it was used by a wide range of biblical literati at various times and thus will turn up in practically all biblical books. Therefore, it can in no way be connected with any specific religious or ideonic trands such as constitute the warp and woof of the "sources" which have been identified by modern scholarship. The application of the *Wiederaufnahme* to the analysis of a biblical composite text is concerned basically with purely literary matters, in the restricted sense of the term. It may be freed from ulterior considerations of theological and similar imports, and thus could provide a new point of departure in the analysis of the biblical books, such as was searched for by Jepsen without convincing results.

In essence, the *Wiederaufnahme* consists of the verbatim or nearly verbatim repetition of a word-cluster, varying in range, at the two intersections at which an independent segment was wedged into a comprehensive textual framework. The main narrative thread which was cut in order to accommodate the insert eventually is resumed by what amounts to a textual echo of the wording which immediately preceded the caesura. The technique was described in detail by C. Kuhl, who introduced the term *Wiederaufnahme* into the historical-critical analysis of biblical literature—predominantly in respect to the Book of Ezekiel—elaborating on M. Wiener's earlier application of the "resumptive repetition" to the structure of the Book of Judges. Neither of these scholars appears to have been aware of some medieval predecessors, such as Rashi, Nachmanides, and Abarbanel, who already had entertained the very same notion, although without presenting the case in a systematic fashion. In their exegesis of ob-viously complex biblical passages, those commentators sometimes have recourse to the formula *ḥāzar ʾel haʿinyan harīʾšōn*, i.e., "he [the author] returns [after the insert] to the first matter on hand," thus employing the precise Hebrew equivalent (*ḥzr ʾl*) of the terms *Wiederaufnahme* and "resumptive repetition." It is to be regretted that neither the pioneering work of the medieval nor that of the modern scholars produced a more widespread utilization of this ancient scribal device towards the clarification of processes which had been at work in the formation of the biblical books in their transmitted configurations.

The application of the *Wiederaufnahme* in attempting to determine the exact extent of the interpolation at 2 Kings 17 produces results which differ from those generally pro-posed. Scholars mostly concur in the identification of Ch. 17 *in toto* as a *compositum* which was secondarily interposed into the already stabilized text of 2 Kings. It may be assumed that in thus delineating the insert they were influenced by the obvious correla-tion with the chapter division. However, here, as in a good number of other instances, the reliability of the chapter division is open to criticism. Some scholars posit the caesura after 2 Kgs 17:6, and have the insert extend from v 7 to the end of the chapter (v 41). One is inclined to assume that in this case the analysis was decided upon by the apparent "annals-character" of 17:1–6, which tallies with a conspicuous characteristic of the Book of Kings not shared by the "insert." In consequence of the lumping together of vv 1–6, a most important indication of the precise demarcation of the interpolated piece was lost, and likewise a clue for the characterization of this interpolation and the rediscovery of the stages by which the present text had accrued. While we concur in the view that the insertion ends with v 41, we propose that its true beginning is to be located in v 5 or, possibly, in v 3. As has been generally recognized, vv 5–6 are a parallel reading of the somewhat differently worded account of the last days of Samaria found in 18:9–11. V 18:9a obviously resumes the historical presentation which broke off after 17:4 (or 17:2) and introduces the "resumptive repetition" of 17:5–6 in 18:9b–11. Disregarding for the present the annals notation 18:1–8, which directly precedes the "resumptive repetition" and which undoubtedly constitutes an integral part of the historiographical framework of Kings, we now can firmly establish the overall enclave to extend from 17:5 (or 17:3) to 17:41.

The composite nature of this enclave is beyond debate. It follows that its constitutive elements must be considered separately. Again, the "resumptive repetition" proves to be of help in drawing the dividing lines between the respective units. Thus, the generally entertained opinion that 17:7–22a form a distinct pericope derives support from the recurrence of the phrase "and he exiled Israel to Assyria" in v 6a, with some variation, in v 23b. The conclusion is buttressed by the employment of the formula "until this day," which will yet require further attention, at the very end of the pericope in 17:23a and 41b; not necessarily to be defined as "resumptive repetitions," they mark off two addi-tional components in the composite insertion, namely, vv 24–33 and 34–41. The resulting complexity is enhanced by various glosses and iterations which cannot be traced here in detail and which in any case do not affect materially our main points of interest.

III

We shall revert now to the annalistic notation in vv 5–6, which, in the above analysis, was effectively isolated from the succeeding text: "The king of Assyria marched against [or: through] the whole country, and he marched up to Samaria and besieged her for three years. In the ninth year of Hoshea, the king of Assyria captured Samaria, exiled Israel to Assyria, and settled them in Ḥalaḥ and Ḥabor, Nehar Gozan, and the cities [G: mountains] of the Medes." This straightforward, factual account does not contain any of the formulaic references to the misdeeds of the Israelite rulers which abound in the Book of Kings and are presented there as the causes of setbacks and disasters which befell their realm. The absence is remarkable and invites an explanation. It is further put in relief by the presence of a negative, although subdued, appreciation of Hoshea's reign in v 2, i.e., in the preceding text unit, which we deem to differ in origin from 17:(3)5–6: "He did what was evil in the sight of the Lord, yet not like the kings of Israel who preceded him." Scholars indeed paid attention to the discrepancy between these two presentations but did not endeavour to provide a more than cursory explanation for it. Thus B. Stade, as quoted by J. A. Montgomery: "The pre-Exilic editor of Kings must . . . have read in the sources at hand notices of Hoshea that presented him in a more favorable light than his predecessors." Similarly, A. Jepsen can find no obvious reason for the "*scheinbar etwas günstigere Urteil über Hosea*" in 17:2 and does not give a single thought to the even more surprising absence of any criticism whatsoever in vv 5–6. Such criticism is absent also from the parallel version of the notation in 18:9–11. However, there the customary severe judgment on Ephraimite kings emerges in an added comment (v 12) which spells out the cause of Samaria's downfall, "because they did not listen to the voice of Yhwh their God, and transgressed his covenant, all that Moses Yhwh's servant had commanded, and did not listen, nor keep it." This verse clearly is a condensed echo of the extensive hortatory passage in 17:7–23, and serves as a redactional link for 18:9–11 (together with 18:1–8) with that piece of paranese.

The doubling of the account of the capture of Samaria, coupled with the deviation of 17:5–6 from the conceptual framework of the Book of Kings, leads to the surmise that this chronistic notation was quoted from a northern source. It may well be a fragment of Ephraimite annals which the Judahite editor of Kings infused into his work for reasons which can no longer be ascertained. The quoting of non-Judahite or even extra-Israelite materials is not an exceptional feature in biblical literature. Suffice it here to draw attention to the Edomite Chronicle in Genesis 36 and the (anti)-Moabite War Song in Num 21:27–30, which most likely was quoted from the probably non-Israelite sayings or songs of the *mošlîm*. This supposition is supported by the additional absence in 17:5–6 of any formula aiming at the synchronization of Hoshea's last years and the fall of Samaria with the regnal years of the contemporaneous Judean king Hezekiah. The omission indeed was noted by scholars, but again is referred to only *en passant*, without an attempt being made to proffer a reasoned explanation of this fact.

The characteristics of the above-defined fragment of an Ephraimite chronicle now can direct us in the search for other pieces of a similar nature in the text complex 17:7–41. What we are looking for are more "factual" accounts which do not exhibit synchronizing formulae or disparaging remarks on matters concerning the northern kingdom, before and after its destruction, sparked by their authors' theological persuasion. With this in mind, we can dispose immediately of two typically parenetic passages, viz., 17:7-23 and 17:34-41, which abound in exactly this type of recrimination. Once these parts are extracted, we are left with the section 17:24-33, which the present text arrangement presents to us as a unit by enclosing it between two mentions of the formula "to this very day" (23bP and 34a). However, also in this pericope two heterogeneous strata may be discerned: one hortatory-interpretative, the other factual. The former consists of vv 25-28 and 32-33. It is at great pains to discredit the foreign-immigrant population by insisting that they adhered to a *cultus mixtus* which consisted of an essentially pagan nucleus, thinly disguised by a transparent Yahwistic veneer. The author's interest lies less in reporting on long-gone-by days than in informing his readers that this objectionable situation had not changed, and was operative "until this day" (v 34a), i.e., until his own times. The latter, "factual" report consists of vv 24 and 29-31. When we now line up all the recovered "factual" pieces in 2 Kings 17, the reconstituted historical account of assumedly Ephraimic provenance would yet lack a suitable introduction. Such an original opening is possibly reflected in vv 3-4, which, like vv 5-6, stand out from the overall historiographical framework by the absence of parenetic and synchronistic formulae. Taking this into account, the basic text of the northern document can approximately be reconstructed as follows:

2 Kgs 17:3   Against him [Hoshea] marched Shalmanezer, king of Assyria; Hoshea submitted to him, and paid him tribute.

4   Then the king of Assyria found out that Hoshea had conspired [against him] by sending messengers to So, the king of Egypt, and did not bring tribute to the king of Assyria [as he had done] year after year.

5   So the king of Assyria marched against [or: through] the whole land, and marched against Samaria and besieged her three years.

6   In the ninth year of Hoshea, the king of Assyria captured Samaria; he exiled Israel to Assyria, and settled them in Ḥalaḥ and Ḥabor, Nehar Gozan, and the cities [G: mountains] of the Medes.

24   [Then] the king of Assyria brought [people] from Babylon and from Kutah, and from ʿAwwa and from Ḥamat and Sefarwaim, and settled [them] in the cities of Samaria in place of the Israelites. They took possession of Samaria and dwelt in her cities.

29   And they worshiped each nation its gods, and put [their idols] in the *bêt habbāmôt* which the Samarians had [built] made, each nation in the cities in which they had settled.

30   The men of Babylon worshiped Sukkōt benōt, and the men of Kut[ah] worshiped Nergal, and the men of Ḥamat worshiped Ashima.

31   The ʿAwwites worshiped Nifḥaz and Tartak, and the Sefarwites burned their children in the fire [as sacrifice] for Adramelek and Anamelek, the gods of Sefarwayim.

The above analysis results in the identification of three major strands interwoven in the text complex 2 Kgs 17:1-18:12:

a. Two annalistic notations exhibiting traits which typify the historiographical framework of the Book of Kings and can be comfortably integrated into it—17:1-4; 18:1-11.

b. Parenetic and hortatory materials characterized by a shared *Gattung* but requiring further internal analysis in order to establish their literary homogeneity or partial hetero-geneity—17:7-22, 25-28, 32-41; 18:12.

The polemic tone of some of the passages included in this group highlight their patently Judean author's intention to interpret the events from his historiosophical point of view. The polemics appear to be aimed at specific groups and at particular historical and religious circumstances. Thus, this text cluster becomes of special importance for an attempted elucidation of the chronological setting in which the final redaction of the comprehensive pericope under discussion was carried out.

c. Fragments of an independent chronistic account of assumedly Ephraimite provenance—17:(3-4), 5-6, 24, 29-31.

IV

The "Northern Chronicle" requires some discussion before we turn to the dating of 2 Kings 17. Its distinctiveness from the other components which were identified rests not only on literary, structural, and ideonic considerations but shows also in some other par-ticularities. They become apparent in the reference to the cultic customs and attitudes of the foreign peoples whom the Assyrian conquerors had brought into the territory of the former northern kingdom, which had been integrated into the Assyrian province system. The basic facts are recorded *sine ira* in vv 29a and 30-31. We are told that "They [the foreigners] worshiped each nation its gods" (29a). This general statement is then broken down into a more detailed roster in which the specific deities of the diverse peoples are enumerated (vv 30-31). In this passage, the foreigners' cults are presented as being pagan throughout. Since "foreign peoples" are involved, this circumstance does not evoke the author's criticism. We find no reference to the reputedly "syncretistic" nature of these cults, exhibiting vestiges of the Yahwistic religion which had been infused into the idol worship. This "accusation" is the very pivot of the "Lions episode." In this short pericope—vv 25-28—the well-known tradition is related which tells of the attacks of lions on the foreign settlers, interpreted by them as a sign of the wrath of Yahweh, caused by the fact that they did not (know how to) worship him. At their request, the king of Assyria authorizes the return of a, or some, priest(s) to the shrine at Bethel, so that the new settlers would receive instruction in the tenets of the Yahwistic creed. The episode has to it the ring of a tradition which may have been native to Bethel, and it is fashioned upon the lion-motif which recurs in several prophetic narratives (1 Kgs 13:24-32; 20:35-36; et al.). When this tradition is set aside, v 29, which follows im-mediately upon it, is rejoined with v 24. Thus, the "factual annals-nucleus" in the text unit 17:24-31 can be identified as consisting of vv 24, 29-31.

Also in this small unit, an editorial gloss can yet be detected. V 29b contains a state-ment which ostentatiously links the foreign cults with "the *bēt habbāmôt* which the Samaritans had made [or: built]." The reference can be only to the central northern sanctuary which Jeroboam I (ben Nebat) had established in Bethel (1 Kgs 12:25-33, cp. ch. 13). The statement most probably stems from the hand of the man who had penned the "Lions episode" or an editor who inserted it into the present context. Like that tale, it purports to conjoin the renewal of the Israelite Bethel cult with the introduction into it of pagan cultic practices. At the same time, the phrase in v 29b may be viewed as a pro-lepsis of the argument developed later in the chapter, to wit, that the combination of the two disparate cult patterns resulted in that seemingly Yahwistic but in truth pagan religion which was yet practiced by the descendants of the foreign settlers in the redactor's times—"until this very day" (vv 32-34a, 41). In essence, the portrayed religious and cultic interpenetration is quite plausible. Such processes may be observed whenever and wherever population changes occur. They can, e.g., be readily traced in the establishment and subsequent development of Israelite shrines on former Canaanite sites after the Conquest of the Land. However, in the case under review, the remark in v 29b most probably is not an integral part of the original Ephraimite document but, rather, an editorial comment. In content it clashes with the immediately following statement that the newcomers established their cults individually, "each nation in the cities in which they had settled." That is to say, they established a variety of shrines, transferring to their new abode the cults to which they had adhered in their diverse homelands. In contradistinction, the phrase "*bēt habbāmôt* which the Samaritans had built" (v 29b) certainly refers to only one Ephraimite *temenos*, namely, to Bethel. There Jeroboam I had established the *bēt habbāmôt* as a singular "high-place-temple," intending it to be the rival Ephraimite sanctuary of the Jerusalem temple. In the original report on Jeroboam's enterprise (1 Kgs 12:31-33), the term *bēt habbāmôt* is always used in the singular to emphasize the uniqueness of the Bethel structure; however, already in the ensuing prophetic tradition, in 1 Kgs 13, the plural *bātê habbāmôt* is employed. In this, as in all subsequent mentions, the plural attests to the Judean writers' and revisers' predisposition to undermine the singularity of the northern *Reichsheiligtum* in Bethel and to relegate it to the status of just one other *bāmāh*. This biased presentation certainly distorts the northerners' understanding of the status of the Bethel shrine. The local hierarchy conceived of it as being "the royal temple, sanctuary of the realm" (Am 7:13), equal in prestige to the royal temple in Jerusalem. Bethel was esteemed by the Ephraimites as the temple of Jerusalem was considered in Judah, as the central, and ultimately the only, legitimate shrine. The predominance of Bethel is reflected in one other editorial comment in 17:32: "and they [i.e., the foreigners, or possibly the remaining Ephraimites] appointed for themselves from among their peers [or: nobles] *bāmôt* priests who officiated at the *bēt habbāmôt*." This comment is a slightly paraphrastic quotation of a distinctive line in the report on Jeroboam I's actions aimed at solidifying his rebellion against the Davidic house and the temple of Jerusalem: "He made [built] the *bēt habbāmôt*, and made [appointed] priests from among the peers [or: nobles] of the people" (1 Kgs 12:31, cp. v 32 and 13:33).

The above analysis leads to the conclusion that the biblical references to the Ephraimite calf cult which propagate the proliferation of the *bēt (bātê) bāmôt* in Samaria, before or after the fall of the northern kingdom, evidence a Judean editorial bias. If, accordingly, the reference of this kind in 17:29b is regarded as secondary to the original wording, the document which relates the importation of foreign settlers and their cults into former Ephraimite territories reads as follows (17:24, 29a, 30, 31):

The king of Assyria brought [people] from Babylon and from Kutah, and from ʿAwwa and from Ḥamat and Sefarwaim, and settled them in the cities of Samaria in place of the Israelites. They took possession of Samaria and dwelt in her cities. And they worshiped each nation its god, each one in the cities in which they settled. . . . The men of Babylon worshiped Sukkōt benōt, and the men of Kut[ah] worshiped Nergal, and the men of Ḥamat worshiped Ashima. The ʿAwwites worshiped Nifḥaz and Tartak, and the Sefarwites burned their children in the fire [as sacrifices] for Adramelek and Anamelek, the gods of Sefarwayim.

V

A closer look at this passage reveals two linguistic particularities which set it apart from the text surrounding it. One of these confers upon this short piece a linguistic uniqueness unparalleled in any other biblical text:

a. The recurrent employment of the verb ʿśh (five times in vv 29–31) with a connotation which differs perceptibly from the prevalent connotations attached to this common root in biblical Hebrew.

b. The use of the toponym "Samaritans," which is not found again either in the Hebrew or the Aramaic biblical onomasticon, and thus is a *hapax legomenon*.

The connotations of ʿśh in biblical Hebrew hardly need to be enumerated here in detail. The root covers a variety of activities all of which equal, in one way or another, *facere*—make, manufacture, fashion, execute, produce, et al. The evidence for the diverse nuances of employment can be easily gathered from any biblical dictionary. Under the comprehensive meaning "to make" can be subsumed also the more specific use of the root in the collocation: "make gods or idols," mostly coupled with a direct object, as, e.g., in Judges 18:24, 31. Somewhat similar is the expression ʿśh zbḥym—to make offerings, or to sacrifice, usually combined with an indirect object (Exod 10:25; 1 Kgs 12:26; cp. Jer 44:19 et al.). By the strength of this prevalent use of ʿśh ʾt, most lexica, commentators, and translations render the phrases in question as "they were making", "they made," taking the plastic representations of the gods, i.e., the idols, to constitute the direct object of the predicates ʿśym, ʿśw. While the value *facere* is perfectly suitable for the translation of the phrase "they set up [G: + their idols] in the *bêt habbāmôt* which the Samaritans had made" which turns up in the gloss in v 29b, its employment in the rendition of the other occurrences of ʿśh in vv 29–31 produces misleading results. The last item in the enumerative list of the pagan cults clearly describes a specific cultic act, a type of sacrifice offered to the deities named—"and the Sefarwites burn their children in the fire [as sacrifices] for Adramelek and Anamelek, the gods of Sefarwayim" (v 31b)—and in no way refers to the making, i.e., the manufacture of images of these deities. The perfect parallelism of this line with the preceding lines forces upon us the conclusion that there ʿśh speaks of the worship of these gods and not of the manufacture of idols. Therefore, these phrases should be rendered: "the Babylonians worship Sukkōt benōt, the Kuthites worship Nergal," etc. The issue was correctly understood by the medieval commentator David Kimchi. In his comment on ʾšr ʿśw hšmrnym, "which the Samaritans had built" (v 29b), and wyhyw ʿśym lhm bbyt hbmwt, "they were making [offering their sacrifices] in the *bêt habbāmôt*," (v 32) he employs the very same verb, ʿśh, found in the text. Against this, he recurrently renders ʿśh in the roster of the foreign cults (vv 29a, 30–31) by the Hebrew root ʿbd, which signifies "worship": "they adhered there [i.e., in Samaria] to the same pagan worship to which they had adhered in their countries [of origin]." It appears that among modern scholars only B. L. Levine captured this correct meaning when commenting on the name Nergal in the *Hebrew Biblical Encyclopedia*: "There . . . [in 2 Kgs 17:30] it is reported that the men of Kutha . . . ʿśw Nergal, that is to say that they worshiped him (*plhw lw*)."

The employment of ʿśh in the above passage, therefore, differs decidedly from its employment in seemingly identical formulae which pertain to the actual fashioning of idols. Examples could be adduced at random. The difference becomes especially prominent when we compare our text with the traditions which report on "the making" of the "golden calf" which, in one way or another, is related to the calf or calves set up by Jeroboam ben Nebat in Bethel (and Dan). In all these cases, the *ʿgl mskh* (Exod 32:48; Deut 9:16; Neh 9:18)—or, in conformity with the "break-up pattern," simply the *ʿgl* (Exod 32:19, 20, 24, 35; Deut 9:21; Hos 8:5) or the *mskh* (Deut 9:12; Hos 13:2, cp. Ps 106:1; further Exod 34:17; Lev 19:4)—constitutes the direct object of *ʿśh*. The quite particular usage of *ʿśh* in 2 Kgs 17:29a, 30-31 elicits the supposition that we encounter here a specifically Ephraimite linguistic trait which possibly mirrors an Akkadian prototype. Akk. *epēšu* exhibits a range of meanings similar to the one which characterizes Hebrew *ʿśh*. Among these we find the connotation "perform a ritual" or "worship," collocated with *pān* or *ana* and the name of a deity or *ilāni*—gods, in general. (It gives me great satisfaction to report that the concurrence of this connotation of Akk. *epēšu* with the unusual employment of Hebrew *ʿśh* in the 2 Kings passage was noted independently by my friend and colleague Hayim Tadmor.) While a possible mediating role of Aramaic in the concurrence of the Hebrew and the Akk. verbs cannot be ruled out, I would not rate its probability very high.

If the proposed interdependence of *ʿśh* in 2 Kgs 17:29a, 30-32 and Akk. *epēšu* can be upheld, the restored "Ephraimite Chronicle" in which these verses are contained could well have an Assyrian antecedent. In other words, the "factual" report on the events which befell Samaria before and after she was taken by the Assyrians, found to be so very different from the historiographical framework of the Book of Kings, possibly emanated from an Akkadian source, handed down to us in an Ephraimite-Hebrew version.

This supposition derives support from the other linguistic particularity to which attention was drawn, in the editorial comment embedded in 17:29. It should be stressed that in this instance we are not concerned with a presumed Ephraimite piece of history-writing but, rather, with a Judean redactional insert. However, in view of the overall concern of 2 Kings 17 with Samaritan history, and as the result of a possible linguistic cross-fertilization, that very short Judean piece appears to exhibit a unique reflex of an Assyrian term. As already mentioned, the toponym "Samaritans," used there in the designation of "the *bêt habbāmôt* which the Samaritans had built," is a *hapax legomenon*. This is the only instance in the Bible in which the (Israelite) inhabitants of the northern kingdom or of the capital, Samaria, are referred to in this manner. This singularity is especially striking in view of the fact that other toponyms derived from the names of countries and cities abound in biblical literature, as can be ascertained by even a cursory perusal of the sources. The absence of the toponym "Samaritan, Samaritans" is conspicuous also in later biblical writings, e.g., in the post-Exilic books, including the Aramaean portions. Whereas we do encounter adjectival constructs like *mlk šmrwn* (1 Kgs 21:1; 2 Kgs 1:3, *et al.*), or *śʿr šmrwn* (1 Kgs 22:10; 2 Kgs 7:1), even Sanballat, the commander of the *ḥyl šmrwn* in Nehemia's days (Neh 3:34), never carries the toponym *šmrwny* but is referred to by another toponym, *ḥrny* (Neh 2:19). It is of interest that also in post-biblical sources the outright toponym *šwmrwnym* is avoided, at least sometimes, even in reference to the Samaritans of the Second Temple Period. Ben-Sira refers to them by the appellation "the foolish people that dwells in Shechem" (B-S 50:26), rather than by a toponym derived from the name Samaria. A similar usage is reflected in one

part of the double Greek translation of 2 Kgs 17:32, which Burney considers to mirror
the original reading, while MT, in his opinion, represents "the restoration of an imperfect text upon the lines of 1 Kgs 12:31." The LXX and Luc. offer there (2 Kgs 17:32)
the reading:

καὶ ἦσαν φοβούμενοι τὸν κύριον. καὶ κατῴκισαν τὰ βδελύγματα αὐτῶν
ἐν τοῖς οἴκοις τῶν ὑψηλῶν ἃ ἐποίησαν ἐν Σαμαρείᾳ ἔθνος ἔθνος ἐν
πόλει ἐν ᾗ κατῴκουσιν ἐν αὐτῇ . . .

It seems that these words reflect the MT of 17:29, with the telling difference that the
toponym *šmrwnym* used there in reference to the building of the *bêt habbāmôt* is
rendered here by the circumscription "which they had built in Samaria."

I tend to assume that the unique appellation *šmrwnym* in 2 Kgs 19:29 possibly
evidences an influence of Assyrian geopolitical terminology on biblical writers. More
probably, it originated in a direct quote from an Assyrian original. I do not take the
name *šmrwnym* to stand for the Assyrian province Samerina, as some commentators
have suggested, but, rather, as a designation of the kingdom of Samaria which the
Assyrians introduced in the days of Adad-Narari III, i.e., approximately 800 BCE. In
the stela from Tell al-Rimah, Adad-Nirari refers to the king of Israel as Ia-'a-su Sa-me-
ri-na-a-a, i.e., Ia'asu the Samarian (1. 8). He similarly designates the Phoenician kings,
"the Tyrian" and "the Sidonian" (1. 9). It is of interest to note that the toponym
"Samarian," applied to the Israelite king, constitutes a departure from the patronymic
Bit-Humri, by which name Adad-Nirari's grandfather, Shalmanesser III, referred to
Jehu, who, in fact, had annihilated the house of Omri. We have no compelling reason to
assume that, as was surmised with respect to the Hebrew term *šmrwnym*, the cuneiform
Sa-me-ri-na-a-a is meant to give expression to the fact that the kingdom of Samaria had
been turned into the Assyrian province Samerina, as was proposed by A. Malamat in a
discussion of Adad-Nirari's stela. Rather should we consider the Hebrew term a one-
time reflection of the toponym "Samarian," used by Adad-Nirari and later by Tiglath
Pileser III in reference to Menachem of Israel, which did not gain for itself a permanent
place in the biblical onomasticon.

VI

Having identified in 2 Kings 17 the remains of an assumed Ephraimite document in
which the last days of Samaria and the settling in the land of foreigners imported by the
Assyrian conqueror had been "factually" recorded, we now return to the questions
posed at the outset of this study: can we yet recapture the diverse stages of adjustments
and annotations which affected that nucleus when it was incorporated into the present
framework? Can we yet establish, even if only in general outlines, the identity of the
revisers, and possibly arrive at some conclusions with regard to the historical conditions
which gave the impetus to the inclusion of the comprehensive enclave in the Book of
Kings?

The key factor in our deliberations on these issues appears to be the editor's manifest
intention to portray a "syncretistic" form of Yahweh worship, yet operative in his own
days and quite obviously rejected by him. His presentation is charged with open

polemics and is aimed at discrediting in the eyes of his readers, most probably his Judean contemporaries, the descendants of those syncretists of old who yet lived in the northern parts of the land of Israel. The need for such an argument surely did not arise ⟶ shortly after the destruction of Samaria. The biblical books give evidence of a rather conciliatory Judean attitude toward the remnants in the northern territories. King Hezekiah attempted to bring about a reconciliation with the erstwhile Ephraimite antagonists of Judah, and he succeeded in his attempt, at least to a measure (2 Chronicles 30). The prophets Jeremiah and Ezekiel seemingly show a preference for the remnants of Ephraim over Judah. A conflict and a clash over matters of political import and of religion and cult indeed did develop in the reign of Josiah, who strove to eradicate the high places in Samaria and especially the central sanctuary in Bethel (2 Kgs 23:16–20), by having recourse to coercion and not to persuasion, as Hezekiah had done. But there is nothing in the reports about his reform which would explain the polemics against the "northern syncretism" which permeate the account in 2 Kings 17. Therefore, I find it difficult to subscribe to the theory recently proposed by M. Cogan that "the destruction of Jerusalem—586 BCE—may serve, then, as the *terminus ad quem* for our polemic." Cogan argues that "Late preexilic Judah, the reign of Josiah, in particular, provides an appropriate setting for attention to be focused upon the Israelite kingdom and its inhabitants, former and present." There is little in the tone of the text under review which would substantiate such a claim. Likewise, I would doubt that 2 Kings 17 turns against "the Israelite exiles, who by their continued idolatry, forfeit any rights to their former inheritance. Our historian denies them legitimacy; their exile is proof of rejection." It would seem that this interpretation of 2 Kings 17 derives from the ascription of the polemic wording to a Deuteronomistic redactor, and from this ascription results the dating of the passage to the time of Josiah.

I would propose that Ch. 17 was incorporated into the Book of Kings at a considerably later stage in the Israelite history, decidedly after the destruction of Jerusalem, and actually after the return from the Exile. Thus, 2 Kings 17 would, in fact, represent one of the latest stages in the editorial processes which affected the Book of Kings. The necessity for the inclusion arose from the post-Exilic author's intent to prevent integration into the returning exiles' community of groups in the Palestinian population who had not shared the experience of the Exile, which had revolutionized the religious attitudes of the deported Judeans. In his view, the local inhabitants, especially of northern Israel, still clung to the disreputable Ephraimite version of the Yahwistic religion, which the prophets had condemned and which he saw as a threat to the purity of the returnees' religious convictions. The danger was enhanced by the fact that the former Israelite population in the north of the country had been infiltrated by "foreign" elements whom the Assyrian had brought there after the destruction of Samaria. Their descendants, who professed an adherence of a sort to the Yahwistic creed, at first attempted to join the returning Exilic community and proposed to rebuild with them the House of God in Jerusalem, asserting that "like you we seek [i.e., revere] your God, and offer him sacrifices" (Ezra 4:1–2). The petitioners are not called there by the comprehensive designation "peoples of the land"—ᶜm hᵓrṣ, ᶜmy hᵓrṣ, or gwyy hᵓrṣwt—the prevalent appelations in the Books of Ezra and Nehemiah of the Palestinians who had not been in exile, but, rather, by the more specific term "adversaries of Judah and Benjamin" (Ezra 4:1).

The insistence of the writer to present his own group as being composed of Judahites and Benjaminites leaves room for the identification of the petitioners as northern Israelites. There is a kernel of truth in their claim that they had been serving the God of Israel and had brought him sacrifices. The traditions which tell of the acceptance of the Jerusalem cult by "men from Asher, Manasseh and Zebulun" in the days of Hezekiah (2 Chron 30:11) and of "men from Shechem, Shiloh, and Samaria," who came up to Judah in the days of Gedaliah, of whose murder they had no knowledge, "carrying offerings and frankincense, to bring to the house of God" (Jer 41:5), reveal the attachment of some northerners to the Jerusalem temple. For this reason, and because of additional considerations of a political and economic nature, some returnees appear to have advocated their acceptance into the newly constituted community. Foremost among them may have been priests who had an obvious interest in increasing the numbers of the faithful who would sustain the service in the rebuilt temple (Hag 2:10–14). The writer of the Ezra passage (4:1–3) objected to this tendency. He took pains to disqualify the petitioning "adversaries of Judah and Benjamin" by putting into their mouths words which disclosed their non-Israelite origins and put in relief their descent from those peoples whom the Assyrians had brought into conquered Samaria. It does not require great powers of discernment to detect the writer's hand in the penning of the petitioners' statement: "we sacrifice to him [to whom this temple is dedicated] from the days that Esarhaddon the king of Assyria had brought us here" (4:2). In the mouths of the petitioners, this statement is incongruous, since it defeats their professed purpose. But it makes excellent sense if we take it to have come from the pen of the antagonistic author who thus wanted to strengthen the hands of the returnees who had decided to reject the approaches of the contaminated inhabitants of northern Palestine.

It stands to reason that from among these circles of post-Exilic Judahites arose the impetus to buttress further the arguments against the acceptance of local Israelites. This purpose was achieved by inserting into the Book of Kings, an "old source," an appropriately worded statement which "proved" that, after the destruction of Samaria, the remaining Israelite population had become unclean due to the infusion into their ranks of ethnically foreign elements, and because of the *cultus mixtus* which had developed, to which the northern population adhered until "this very day" (2 Kgs 17:34, 41), that is to say, until the days of the return from the Exile.

The Case of the Suspected Adulteress, Numbers 5:11-31: Redaction and Meaning

JACOB MILGROM

Modern critics uniformly regard the text of the law of the suspected adulteress (Num 5:11-31) as a conflation of at least two sources. Two procedures are employed to test the suspect, an oath and an ordeal (16-24, 27-28), with a sacrifice perhaps constituting a third test (15, 25-26). Moreover, repetitions abound (16b = 8a; 19a = 21a; 21b = 22a; 24a = 26b = 27a; 12b-14 = 29f.).[1] Notwithstanding this evidence for multiple sources, it is to the merit of two recent scholars, M. Fishbane and H. C. Brichto, that they see this text as a logical and unified composition.[2] It is submitted that their conception of the text is correct, with the exception of two additions, verses 21 and 31, which, however, provide the key to unlock the redaction and meaning of the text.

THE SUSPECTED ADULTERESS, NUM 5:12-31

A. *The Case*, 12-14
   1. outside suspicion, 12-13
   2. husband's suspicion, 14

   B. *Preparation of the Ritual-Ordeal*, 15-18
      1. *minḥāh*, 15
      2. water, 17
      3. woman, 18 (16)

      C. *The Oath-Imprecation*, 19-24
         1. oral adjuration, 19-22
         [interpolation, 21]
         2. written adjuration dissolved and to be imbibed, 23-24

   B'. *Execution of the Ritual-Ordeal*, 25-28
      1. *minḥāh*, 25-26a
      2. water, 26b
      3. woman, effect on, 27-28

---

1. E.g., G. B. Gray, *Numbers* (I.C.C., 1903) pp. 43-49; Baentsch, *Exodus, Leviticus and Numeri (HKAT,* 1903), pp. 363-64.

2. M. Fishbane, "Accusations of Adultery: A Study of Law and Scribal Practice in Numbers 5:11-31," *HUCA* 45 (1974); 25-45; H. C. Brichto, "The Case of the Sota and a Reconsideration of Biblical Law," *HUCA* 46 (1975); 55-70.

A'. *The Case*, 29-30 (resumptive subscript framed by inverse inclusion)
1. outside suspicion, 29
2. husband's suspicion, 30
[postscript, 31]

The unity of the text is projected into clear relief by its structure. As can be seen by the diagram, it consists of five sections arranged in introverted (chiastic) order. The facts of the case begin and end the text (12-14, A; 29-30, A') and contain the following common elements: *tiśṭeh ᵓiššāh* (29, 12), *niṭmᵊᵓāh* (29, 12, 13, 14), *taʿăbōr ʿālā(y)w rûaḥ qinᵊᵓāh* (30, 14) and *qinnē ᵓet ᵓištô* (30, 14). Though the closing statement (A') is only a summary of the case, it nevertheless articulates all its essential elements: the wife's straying and defilement and the husband's suspicions. The exact nature of the charges levied against the accused are not easily decipherable and their elucidation is not really germane to this paper. Tentatively, the hypothesis of M. Fishbane[3] will be accepted—that in view of a similar case in Codex Hammurabi, two situations are predicated: the woman has aroused suspicion in the community (12b-13, 29; cf. CH 132) or the suspicion has originated with her husband (14, 34; cf. CH 131). Bifurcation along these lines is clearly evident in the closing statement, A', but the initial *waw* of verse 14 in the opening formulation A will have to be rendered as "or."

The introverted structure of this text is projected in the clearest relief by comparing the preparation and execution sections of the ritual-ordeal (15-18, B; 25-28, B'). First, these sections contain common expressions: *minḥat qᵊnāᵓôt* (25, 15, 18), *ᵓazkārātāh/ mazkeret/zikkārôn* (26, 15, 18), *wᵊlāqaḥ hakkōhēn* (25, 17), *lipnê YHWH* (25, 16, 18), and *wᵊhiqrîb ᵓōtāh* (25, 16). Second, the structure of the components of each section is identical: *minḥāh*-water-woman. The recognition of this similar substructure clarifies two ostensible anomalies. First, the text ostensibly states that the woman was placed before the altar (16) before the preparation of the water (17). However, by using a repetitive resumption (18a), the author thereby indicates that the waters were prepared by the priest prior to the placement of the woman before the altar. The structure indicates the same sequence both in the preparation and in the execution: the woman's role follows that of the water. Second, the purpose of verses 27-28 is now seen in proper perspective. These verses are not just an editorial summation or a "prognosis,"[4] but again, in keeping with structural symmetry, they provide a kinetic counterpart to the static picture of verse 18. Both passages find the woman standing before the altar. In verse 18 she holds the *minḥāh* in her hands; in verses 27-28 the waters are working their effect within her.

Sections B and B' reveal another inverse symmetry, not in language but in procedure, as illustrated in the diagram on the following page.[5]

The *minḥāh* offering brought by the woman or, rather, by the husband on her behalf (15) is of the cheapest edible grain, barley (cf. 2 Kgs 7:1), and it is deprived of the otherwise two essential elements of the *minḥāh*, the oil and frankincense (Lev ch. 2). During the oath it remains in the hands of the woman; thereafter, in a dedicatory rite it is transferred by the priest to the altar, i.e., to the realm of God. The ordeal water

3. "Accusations," pp. 35-38.
4. Ibid.
5. This Lévi-Straussian model was suggested to me by Shalom Feldblum in a graduate seminar given at the Hebrew University.

The Ritual-Ordeal

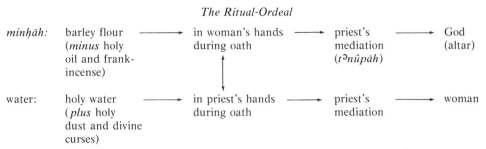

undergoes a procedure symmetrically opposite to the *minḥāh*. It originates in God's realm, the sanctuary laver, from which the priest draws forth the water. In contrast to the two elements *withdrawn* from the woman's *minḥāh*, two elements are *added* to the water to increase its sanctity and, hence, its efficacy—i.e., the dust from the sanctuary floor and the written oath containing the divine name. During the recitation of the adjuration, this water is in the priest's hands while the woman holds the *minḥāh* in her hands. The priest then transfers the woman's *minḥāh* to the sacred realm of the altar and transfers the sacred water to the profane realm of the woman's body. Thus the introversion is symmetrically balanced: the priest is the medium by which both the woman's profane offering is dedicated to the Lord and the divinely empowered water enters her profane body.

The middle section (19–24, C), the oath, is the pivot of the entire structure and, hence, its most important section. Its verbal elements tie it to all the other sections. Thus, it twice repeats the following elements from A, and in chiastic order: *šākab ʾîš ʾōtāk*, *śāṭît, ṭumᵊʾāh* (19–20, 12–13), and from B it repeats *mê hammārîm hamᵊārᵊrîm* (19, 24, 18). From B' it borrows *hammayim hamᵊārᵊrîm lᵊmārîm* (27, 24), *wᵊṣābᵊtāh biṭnāh wᵊnāplāh yᵊrēkāh* (27, 21, 22), *ʾālāh bᵊqereb ʿammāh* (27, 21), *wᵊniqqᵊtāh* (28, 19), *wᵊniṭmᵊʾāh* (27, 28, 19, 20), and from A' *tiśṭeh taḥat ʾîšāh* and *niṭmᵊʾāh* (29, 19, 20). The conditions of the curse are stated in negative form before the positive (19, 20), but in their recapitulation they appear in reverse order (27, 28).

Section C exhibits inner cohesion through the use of introverted or chiastic phraseology. Thus the element of *šākab* in the adjuration begins the negative statement of the oath and ends its positive restatement (19–20). The oath-curse, *šᵊbuʿāh-ʾālāh*, mentioned twice in 21, is also introverted. Moreover, the compound expression for the ordeal water, "spell-inducing *mārîm* water" (19, 24), is not only introverted (in the last verse in which it occurs, 24) but is also broken into single components, "spell-inducing water" (22) and "*mārîm* water" (23). Thus every possible permutation of this compound is accounted for.

Yet it is patently clear that section C is inflated because of the intrusion of verse 21. Not only is the notice that the priest adjures the woman repeated here (19aα, 21aα) but also the content of the adjuration (21b, 22a). Thus, the beginning and end of the oath are not clearly demarcated in the text, the result being that both the Mishnah (Sot 2:3) and Philo (Laws 3:60) acknowledge differences of opinion concerning its exact wording. Nevertheless, there can be little doubt that originally 22 followed 20, for then the adjuration reads smoothly and lucidly: " . . . If a man other than your husband has had carnal relations with you may this water that induces the spell enter your body causing the belly to distend and the thigh to sag. . . . " Furthermore, even if the redundancies of 21 could be justified there is no way of harmonizing the jarring and abrasive juxtaposition of 22 to 21, which would imply that first her physical condition will make her a byword and then she will drink the water. However, it is clear that the sagging thigh and distended belly are not the cause but the effect of the water. Hence instead of the sequential verb *ûbāʾû*, "May [this water] enter" (22), one would have expected the infinitive construct *bᵊbôʾ*, "As [this water] enters," the same construction as the previous *bᵊtēt*, "As [the Lord] causes" (21).[6] However, *ûbāʾû* follows both logically and grammatically after 20, for then the prescribed ordeal is a consequence of the accusation.

Fortunately, the reason for the interpolation of 21 is not difficult to discern. Without it, the adjuration contains no mention of the name of God, and the formula gives the impression that the powers of the curse inhere in the water. It was therefore essential to add 21 to the adjuration in order to emphasize that the imprecation derives its force not from the water but from the Lord. It may therefore be conjectured that originally the present formula (minus 21) was an ancient Near Eastern incantation for an ordeal employing magical water which did not invoke the name of any deity.[7] It may have been incorporated into the Israelite cult at local high places or shrines and converted into an oath by having the suspected adulteress respond "amen" (22b). The priestly legislator, however, found the formula unacceptable, since it ostensibly attributed the effect of the oath to the water itself. Since the formula was already accepted and in widespread use he would have incurred too much resistance had he attempted to alter its wording. Instead he followed the simple and more acceptable expedient by adding a statement affirming that the efficacy of the oath was due to the God of Israel (21b). And to forestall the protest that no change in the text was necessary, since an oath implied the invocation of the Deity, he also added a new thought, namely, that the convicted adulteress would become a byword among her people (21a; cf. Jer 29:22).

The wording of these two clauses that now comprise the text of the oath in 21 was made to fit artistically and coherently with the rest of the oath formula. Thus the Lord will *yittēn* (21), make her a byword in response to *her (way)yittēn*, allowing a man other than her husband to have carnal relations with her (20b). Also, the effect of the imprecation (21b) is given in the reverse order of 22a, the thigh preceding the belly, again providing a chiastic balance. Another chiasm was produced within 21 with the words "oath," *šᵊbûʿāh*, and "imprecation," *ʾālāh*. Finally, the repetition of the instruction to the priest (21a) was added, underscoring the fervent insistence of the legislator that this new element be added to the imprecation. Of course, it is this repetition which fully exposes the interpolation, but it is even more tellingly betrayed, as already indicated, by the discrepancy in the order of events: the effect ostensibly anticipates the cause, i.e., first we are informed that she will become a byword (21b) and only afterward that her condition will be caused by the water (22a).

Nonetheless, there can be no doubt that the interpolation of 21 took place during the early formation of the text and not during its final stages—this for the compelling reason that the clause stating that the guilty woman will become an object of derision (21a) is also present in the execution section (27b). Indeed, the presence of the byword in the execution passage (B′) presumes that it was already an element of the adjuration (C).

---

6. Ezek 5:15b–16 affords an exact analogy when the announcement of the punishment in the infinitive *baʿăśôtî* and *bᵊšallᵊḥî* is also written *after* the identical effect, i.e., Israel becoming a byword (15a).

7. E.g., E. Reiner, *Šurpu*, *AFO*, Beiheft II (Graz, 1968), cols. III, IX.

There is a second interpolation in the text that needs to be explained: the postscript of 31. That it is a postscript and is not an organic part of the text is clear from the structure of the final section (29–30, A'). The section is encased by an inverted inclusion *zōʾt tôrat . . . hattôrāh hazzōʾt* (cf. also 6:21). Thus, in thought and in form, the law of the suspected adulteress is finished and sealed by this concluding inclusion. What, then, is the purpose of the postscript of verse 31? First, let us understand its meaning. The first half, *wᵊniqqāh hāʾîš mēʿāwōn*, "the husband shall be free from punishment," is clearly addressed to the husband; it is to assure him that he has nothing to lose by bringing his wife to the ordeal. His suspicions will either be proven or laid to rest, and in the latter case a harmonious relationship may be restored. The second half of the verse, *wᵊhāʾiššāh hahiwʾ tiśśāʾ ʾet ʿăwōnāh*, "that woman shall suffer her punishment," would seem to be addressed to the suspected adulteress. Understood this way, however, this addendum is a pointless redundancy.[8] However, one should not forget that the idiom *nāśāʾ ʿāwōn* implies that she is punished through divine agency (e.g., Lev 5:1, 17; 7:18, 17:16; 19:8; 20:17, 19; Num 9:13 [with the synonym *ḥēṭʾ*]; 14:34; 30:16.[9] Thus, this clause is not addressed to the woman but to her husband and community; it reminds them that if the adulteress is convicted by the ordeal, her punishment rests not with them but solely with God. And this brings us to the very heart of the matter concerning the purpose of this ritual and its place within biblical jurisprudence. It confronts us with the glaring paradox postulated by this ritual: the adulteress, proven guilty by the ordeal, namely, by God Himself, is not punished with death! True, her punishment is just, "poetically" just. She who opened herself to illicit seed is doomed to be permanently sterile. Yet the gnawing question still remains: having been proven guilty of adultery, why is she not summarily put to death?

The magnitude of this question reaches its full limits when Israel's law of adultery is compared with that of its neighbors. Ancient Near Eastern law—except for the Bible—allows the husband to mitigate or even waive the death penalty against the adulterer.[10] In Israel, however, the death sentence may not be commuted. All biblical sources agree that the prohibition against adultery was incorporated into the national covenant at Sinai to which every Israelite swore allegiance (Exod 24:1–8; Deut 5:24–26) and all subsequent generations were bound (Deut 29:9–14). Indeed, when both Hosea and Jeremiah score Israel for violating the Sinaitic covenant they specify the sin of adultery (e.g., Hos 4:2; Jer 7:9). The testimony of Jeremiah is particularly striking, since he expressly pinpoints adultery as the cause of Israel's national doom (Jer 5:7–9; 7:9–15; 29:23a). Thus in Israel the inclusion of adultery in the Sinaitic covenant guaranteed legal consequences. Adultery had to be punished with death, else God would destroy the

---

8. The rabbis take advantage of the ambiguity for their ethical purposes: "only if the husband is himself clear of sin will his wife suffer her punishment," i.e., the ordeal will only work in the case of an impure wife of a pure husband (Sifre, Numbers, 21). It was probably this rabbinic teaching that prompted Jesus to decide in the case of an apprehended adulteress: "he that is without sin among you, let him be the first to cast a stone at her" (John 8:2ff.). She indeed was released, not because Jesus' appeal touched the assembly's conscience but because he cited the law; cf. D. Daube, "Biblical Landmarks in the Struggle for Women's Rights," *The Judicial Review* 23 (1978): 177–97.

9. Cf. W. Zimmerli, "Die Eigenart der prophetischen Rede des Ezechiel," *ZAW* 66 (1954): 1–26.

10. E.g., CH 129; MAL 14–16; LH 192f.; cf. Pritchard, *Ancient Near Eastern Texts* (Princeton, 1950), pp. 171, 181, 196.

malefactors and, indeed, the entire community which had allowed it to go unpunished. Why, then, is the adulteress convicted by the ordeal, i.e., by God Himself, permitted to escape death?

The key to the answer, I submit, lies in the fact that the guilty woman was *unapprehended by man*. That this element is the most significant in her case is shown by the fact that it is cited four times in her indictment, each in a different manner: (1) *wᵊneʿᵃlam mēʿēynê ʾîšāh*, "unbeknown to her husband"; (2) *wᵊnistᵊrāh*, "she keeps secret" (or "it was done clandestinely"); (3) *wᵊhîʾ loʾ nitpāśāh*, "without being apprehended"; (4) *wᵊʿēd ʾên bāh*, "and there is no witness against her" (v 13). These clear redundancies, among others, lead one critic to assert that their purpose is "to give weight to what might (and all too correctly!) be seen as a transparent charade . . . to protect the woman as wife in the disadvantaged position determined for her by the mores of ancient Israel's society."[11] This stylistic inflation, however, may have been deliberately written with a judicial purpose in mind: to emphasize the cardinal principle that the unapprehended criminal is not subject to the jurisdiction of the human court. Since the adulteress has not been apprehended—as the text repeats with staccato emphasis—then the community and, especially, the overwrought husband may not give way to their passions to lynch her. Indeed, even if proven guilty by the ordeal, they may not put her to death. God has provided that the punishment be built into the ordeal and there is no need for human mediation. Unapprehended adultery, a sin against man (the husband) and God, remains punishable only by God, and that punishment is inherent in the ordeal.

Supportive evidence may also be adduced from the absence of the technical verb for committing adultery, *nāʾap*, which is found in the Decalogue (Exod 20:15; Deut 5:17) and the Priestly Code itself (e.g., Lev 20:10, four times in this one verse!). Thus, though the legislator expressed the woman's infidelity in four different ways, it may be no accident that he refrained from using the legal term *nāʾap*, for he wished to disassociate this woman's fate from the death penalty imposed for adultery. The glaring omission of the term *nāʾap* is, then, but another indication that her punishment lies outside the human court.

There is yet another consideration which buttresses this conclusion. It has been shown in cross-cultural studies that societies will resort to ordeals when the people at large suspect an individual of committing an infraction which endangers the whole community. In such a situation a quick and decisive verdict is necessary. The prolonged procedures of judicial investigation or the awaiting of divine retribution in the case of a false oath cannot be tolerated.[12] But what danger does the suspected adulteress pose to her community that would mandate an immediate decision by God? Surely it cannot be that she violated one of the commandments of the Decalogue. If so, the ordeal would have been instituted for other suspected covenantal infractions, e.g., idolatry, Sabbath violation, thievery. However, the fact remains that the ordeal is prescribed for the suspected adulteress and for no other case! The reason, then, must be sought in the dreaded consequences which the priestly law wishes to forestall at all costs: that she be lynched by mob rule or its legal equivalent, a kangaroo court.

A word needs to be said concerning the penalty itself. Whereas man has no choice but

11. Brichto, "The Sota."
12. Cf. T. Frymer, "Studies in Trial by River Ordeal" (diss. Yale, 1976), pp. 1–59.

to put the apprehended adulteress to death, God metes out a more precise retribution. It is called the measure-for-measure principle, poetic justice, custom-made for each criminal in order to make the punishment precisely fit the crime. For example, Jacob, who deceived Esau with a goatskin garment (Gen 27:16), is himself deceived by a similar garment (Gen 37:31–35). God's sentence that Israel must wander forty years in the wilderness is retribution for the forty days the spies spent in the Holy Land gathering their demoralizing data (Num 14:33f.; see also Ezek 4:4-6). So the adulteress who acquiesced to receive forbidden seed is doomed to sterility for the rest of her life.[13] The ordeal clearly presumes belief in its efficacy, to wit: the guilty woman would be so fearful of its consequences that she would rather confess than subject herself to its dreaded consequences. Thus at an attested river ordeal in Mari, one of the litigant's representatives drowns in the "River-god." He then requests that the lives of his three remaining representatives be spared the ordeal and he will renounce his claim.[14].

Finally, that the suspected adulteress is not put to death either by man or God provides the necessary clue to explain how an ordeal with its inherent magical and pagan elements was allowed to enter the legislation of the Torah, or to answer the paradox as it was phrased by Nachmanides (*ad loc.*): this is the only case in biblical law where the outcome depends on a miracle. The answer, I submit, is inherent in the ordeal: it provides the priestly legislator with an accepted practice by which he can remove the jurisdiction and punishment of the unapprehended adulteress from human hands and thereby guarantee that she will not be put to death.

This, then, is the meaning of the subscript, verse 31. It encourages the suspicious husband to bring his wife to the ordeal by promising him complete exoneration if his suspicions are proven unfounded, and it also reminds him and the rest of his community *wᵊhāʾiššāh hāhiwʾ tiśśāʾ ʾet ʿăwōnāh*, that since the woman's alleged crime was unapprehended by man, she is removed from the jurisdiction of man.

If this subscript is a gloss, as the structure of the text has indicated, it is a correct one. Its author has understood the thrust of this law and its place in biblical jurisprudence, and by inserting it he has made sure that we will understand it too.

In sum, the biblical law of the suspected adulteress provides a unique example of how the priestly legislators made use of a pagan ordeal in order to protect a suspected but unproven adulteress from the vengeance of an irate husband or community by mandating that God will decide her case.

---

13. The rabbis reveal great ingenuity in discovering other instances of measure-for-measure punishment in her case: cf. Num R. 9:24; Tosef Sot 3:1-19.

14. Cf. G. Dossin, "L'ordalie à Mari," *Comptes rendus de l'Académie des Inscriptions et Belle-Lettres* (1958): 387–92.

The Anticipatory Use of Information as a Literary Feature of the Genesis Narratives

NAHUM M. SARNA

The subject of this paper relates to one particular aspect of the process by which the collection of individual narratives in the Book of Genesis achieved their final form as a unified whole. Specifically, I refer to a little-noted phenomenon that recurs with a fair degree of frequency, namely, the sudden introduction into a text of certain information which is extraneous to the immediate context but which is later seen to be crucial to the understanding of a subsequent episode or theme.

As far as I know, the first to draw attention to this was Rashi's grandson, the renowned exegete Rabbi Samuel b. Meir, known by the acronym RaShBaM (Rashbam, c. 1080-c. 1175 C.E.). In his comment to Gen 1:1 he writes, "It is a characteristic of the Scriptures anticipatively to present an irrelevant item for the sake of the subsequent context."[1] He then goes on to illustrate his point by citing, among others, the case of Gen 9:18: "The sons of Noah who came out of the ark were Shem, Ham and Japheth—Ham being the father of Canaan." Now Noah's sons have previously been thrice listed[2] without the additional remark, which is quite beside the point in a context dealing solely with the three sons who emerged from the ark after the Flood, and through whom the earth was repopulated. The information about Canaan's relationship to Ham is repeated in v 22, again without immediate relevancy.

It is obvious that mention of Canaan in these two passages is connected with the succeeding narrative about Noah's drunkenness and the accompanying shameful act perpetrated by Ham, as a consequence of which Noah lays a curse upon Canaan. Modern commentators mostly take it for granted that the note about Ham being the father of Canaan is a gloss introduced into the text by a compiler or editor for the purpose of smoothing the transition from vv 18f. to 20ff. At first glance, Rashbam appears to give the same explanation, in that he takes the note to be a necessary clarification of the identity of Canaan, who is about to be cursed. Without it, the reader would not know who this Canaan is or what he had to do with Ham who was the guilty party. Yet there is a fundamental difference between the perception of the Rashbam and the views of modern commentators. Whereas the latter relate to the note solely in terms of its immediately limited function within the specific pericope, Rashbam treats it from a broader perspective. To him it is one instance among several of an original, characteristic feature of the Narrator's literary technique, not a harmonizing gloss linking P and J materials.

It seems to me that there are some arguments that can be brought in favor of

1. D. Rosin, ed. (Breslau, 1882; reprinted New York, 1949), pp. 3f., commentary to Gen 1:1.
2. 5:32; 6:10; 7:13.

Rashbam's general observation. Admittedly, the story of the curse upon Canaan is replete with difficulties. We are left uncertain as to the precise nature of Ham's offense, whether v 22 is to be taken literally or as a euphemism for some act of gross immorality.[3] We do not know why Ham is described here as "the youngest son" (v 24) when, in fact, all the lists uniformly make him Noah's second son. And, most difficult of all, we are not told why Noah cursed Canaan, Ham's son, rather than Ham himself.[4] One thing is certain: whatever happened to Noah, the biblical account of the experience has been thoroughly emasculated. Even as Shem and Japhet virtuously covered the nakedness of their father, so the narrator piously concealed from posterity the sordid details of the shameful incident, leaving us only a very truncated version and thus causing the insuperable difficulties of the present narrative. Incidentally, the same reticence and the same concision characterize the story of Reuben's sexual transgression.[5]

Be all this as it may, the fact of Canaan's Hamite paternity clearly had great significance for the narrator or redactor; otherwise it would not have been reiterated within the short space of five verses. Moreover, one may rightly wonder why the entire episode is told in the first place.[6] What role does it play within the wider story of Noah or, indeed, within the complex of pre-Abrahamic narratives? The answer is that it introduces one of the major themes of the Pentateuch, one which is repeated in one form or another several times in Genesis.

The Table of Nations, which appears in the following chapter, presents both Egypt and Canaan as sons of Ham (10:6). In other texts, Egypt is equated with Ham. Such is the case in Ps 78:51, which describes the last of the plagues:

> He struck every firstborn of Egypt,
> the first fruits of their vigor in the land of Ham.

In Pss 105:23, 27; 106:22 the identity is even more specific, Egypt being designated "the land of Ham." The close association between Ham/Egypt and Canaan undoubtedly has an historical basis. It harks back to that period when Canaan was a province of Egypt, i.e., in the course of the Late Kingdom, under the 18th and 19th dynasties (c. 1550–1200 B.C.E.).[7] The expression of political relationships in terms of genealogies constructed along familial lines is, of course, a well-recognized and recurring feature of Genesis. "Canaan" in 9:18, 22 is representative of the population group, at this time under Egyptian suzerainty. The curse on Canaan, invoked in response to an act of moral depravity, is the first intimation of the theme of the corruption of the Canaanites, which is given as the justification for their being dispossessed of their land and for the transfer of that

---

3. Whether Ham was guilty of castrating his father or of practising sodomy upon him is discussed in Sanh 70a. On the basis of Lev 20:11, S. Gevirtz, "A Father's Curse," *Mosaic* 2/3 (1969): 56–61, believes that Ham violated his father's wife. However, what is described in Gen 9:22–23 would be hard to reconcile with such an explanation.

4. Saadiah (882–942 C.E.) takes "Canaan" in vv 25, 26 as though it read "father of Canaan." This is followed by Jonah ibn Janah, *Sefer Ha-Riqmah*, ed. M. Wilensky (Berlin, 1930), I, p. 265, line 8, and by Prophiat Duran in his *Maase Efod*, ed. J. Friedländler and J. Kohn (Vienna, 1865), p. 150.

5. 35:22; on which, see below.

6. For an historical explanation, see D. Neiman, "The Date and Circumstances of the Cursing of Canaan," in *Biblical Motifs*, ed. A. Altmann, *Brandeis University Texts and Studies*, Vol. III (Cambridge, Massachusetts, 1966), pp. 113–34; A. Van Selms, "Judge Shamgar," *VT*, XIV (1964): 294–309.

7. See R. de Vaux, *The Early History of Israel*, trans. David Smith (Philadelphia, 1978), pp. 82–123.

land to the descendants of Abraham. This reason is explicitly stated in Lev 20:23f. following a list of sexual abominations:

> You shall not follow the practices of the nation that I am driving out before you. For it is because they did all these things that I abhorred them and said to you: You shall possess their land. . . .

A similar reason is given in 18:24f. This verdict concludes another long list of prohibitions dealing with sexual relations which, significantly, begins as follows (v 3): "You shall not copy the practices of the land of Egypt where you dwelt, or of the land of Canaan to which I am taking you." Egypt and Canaan are coupled together as being equally guilty of moral perversion. This self-same theme is behind several episodes in the Book of Genesis: Pharaoh's treatment of Sarah (12:10-20), Abimelech's dealings with her (ch. 20), the sexual immorality of the Sodomites (19:5-8), Dina's experience with the Canaanite prince of Shechem (ch. 34), the sexual offenses of Er and Onan, sons of Judah's Canaanite wife (ch. 35), and, finally, Potiphar's wife's attempted seduction of Joseph in Egypt (ch. 39).

In light of all the above, it is pertinent to raise the question of whether the contextually irrelevant remark in 9:18, 22 as to Ham's paternity of Canaan is simply a gloss, or whether it is a literary device deliberately introduced into the text in order to insinuate, first, the identity of the Canaan who is about to be cursed—a true son of Egypt!,[8] and, second, the Canaanites in general, a people whose depravity is a major theme of Genesis because it provides the moral justification for their displacement by the descendants of the patriarchs. The answer to this question will depend upon the cumulative effect of the frequency with which this anticipatory device is found in the Genesis narratives. Let us therefore consider some more examples.

The genealogy of Shem is listed in Gen 11:10-32, where it serves to close the gap between Noah and Abraham. The individual generations are given, all in identical formulaic language, until one arrives at v 26, when the pattern is suddenly varied. Hitherto, only the chief descendant has been noted, while other children are anonymously dismissed with the prosaic observation that the aforementioned "begot sons and daughters." In Terah's case, all three sons are named. This departure from the norm clearly indicates that a turning point in history has been reached, and this impression is reinforced by the introduction of the ᵓelleh tôlᵊdōt formula in v 27 and the repetition of the information of v 26, except that this time we are supplied with the additional intelligence that "Haran begot Lot" and that he died young, before the exodus from Ur of the Chaldeans (v 28).

It cannot be accidental that every one of these facts is essential to the understanding of subsequent developments in the biographies of Abraham and his offspring. Nahor need be mentioned because his name recurs repeatedly in connection with Isaac's marriage and Jacob's flight from Esau. Abraham's servant travels to "the city of Nahor" (24:10), where he meets Rebekah, who is of the family of "Abraham's brother Nahor" (v 15), and the girl identifies herself as "the daughter of Bethuel son of Milcah whom she bore to Nahor" (v 24), a fact repeated by the servant later on (v 47). Jacob flees Esau's wrath to find shelter with "Laban the son of Nahor" (29:5), and "the god of Nahor" appears in the treaty concluded between him and his uncle (31:53). Lot has to be introduced because he is soon to be reported as traveling with Abraham (11:31; 12:5), and his being

---

8. So noted by Abraham ibn Ezra in his comment to Gen 9:18.

orphaned explains in advance why this happened.[9] In other words, all the data contained in 11:27–28 is anticipatory and integral to the drama yet to unfold.

But this is not all. There are other anomalous aspects of the genealogy of Terah. The names of the wives of Abram and Nahor are recorded (11:29), but not that of Haran; Sarai is indisputably the more important of the two women, yet, most strangely, her parentage is omitted while Milcah's is given; Sarai is described as being "barren" (v 30), but not so Milcah, even though she too has no children. Here again, every item can be seen to be crucial to the subsequent narratives. Haran's wife is ignored because she plays no role in the patriarchal lives, while Milcah will be encountered again by virtue of her being Rebekah's grandmother.[10] The preclusion of any information about the matriarch's forebears is so extraordinary that it must be deliberate and purposeful. It seems to me that this phenomenon can be satisfactorily explained only on the presumption of a foreknowledge of the encounter with Abimelech, as told in ch. 20. On that occasion, Abraham made the self-justifying claim that Sarah was truly his sister, i.e., his father's daughter, though not his mother's (20:12).[11] In the earlier confrontation with Pharaoh, Abraham did not respond to the king's query, "Why did you say, 'She is my sister'?" because he is summarily expelled from the realm. In this instance, Abimelech insists on an answer (20:9), and the reader wonders how Abraham will extricate himself from his embarrassing predicament. Had Sarah's parentage been disclosed in the genealogy of ch. 11, the story of ch. 20 would have been divested of its suspense, with its literary qualities and effect being gravely impaired as a result. Finally, the designation of the matriarch as "barren" is intended, as von Rad has noted, "not only to prepare the reader for the event that is conditioned by this fact, but, above all, to make him conscious of the paradox of God's initial speech to Abraham."[12] How can God's promises be fulfilled if the patriarch's wife is barren?[13] Of course, barrenness is a major motif of the patriarchal narrative cycles, one expression of the still larger *Leitmotif*, the interplay between divine promise and frustrating reality. In sum, the genealogy must be seen as being inseparable from the narratives.

Still another example of the literary technique of introducing a parenthetic note not

9. M. Noth, *A History of Pentateuchal Traditions* (Englewood Cliffs, New Jersey, 1972), trans. Bernhard W. Anderson, p. 13 and n. 28, observes that in 12:4a, which he assigns to J (p. 28), Lot appears suddenly with no introduction. The narrative is thus regarded as being fragmentary. He postulates that Gen 11:28–30 was inserted into the appendix of 11:27, 31, 32 [P] in order to provide certain specific details. It would appear to be simpler to explain the absence of an explanatory note about Lot in 12:4 as being unnecessary in light of the information already given in 11:27–31.

10. Gen 22:20, 23; 24:15, 24, 47.

11. This claim must be taken seriously. It is hardly likely to be the invention of a writer who was sensitive to the idea of Abraham resorting to falsehood even though in self-defense. The later the authorship of the passage, the less the likelihood of a writer inventing a tale ascribing to the patriarch a practice abhorrent to the sexual morality of Israel as expressed in the legal codes (Lev 18:9, 11; 20:17; Deut 27:22; cf. Ezek 22:11). Furthermore, to invent a claim of Sarah being a half-sister in order to save Abraham from telling a lie is to accept the preposterous conclusion that an incestuous marriage is a lesser offense, something of which no biblical writer could have been guilty. As a matter of fact, the veracity of the claim of 20:12 is reinforced by the independently attested preference of the Terahites for endogamy. Thus, Nahor marries his niece (10:24); Isaac marries the granddaughter of Abraham's brother (24:3ff.); the ostensible reason for sending Jacob to Paddan-aram is to find a wife among Rebekah's family (28:1f.), and the man indeed marries two cousins, something that Laban finds desirable (29:19).

12. G. von Rad, *Genesis*, O.T.L., trans John H. Marks (Philadelphia, 1961), p. 154.

13. Cf. Gen 15:2.

immediately germane to the subject at hand, but whose significance later becomes apparent, is to be found in ch. 13 in connection with the separation of Lot from Abraham. In selecting for himself choice grazing land, Lot observed that the whole plain of the Jordan was well watered "all the way to Zoar, like the garden of the LORD, like the land of Egypt" (13:10). The sequence of the thought, however, is interrupted by the remark, "this was because the LORD destroyed Sodom and Gomorrah." At the end of the narrative another note has been appended, to the effect that "the inhabitants of Sodom were very wicked sinners against the LORD" (v 13). It hardly requires much imagination to see that both observations are preparatory to the events of chs. 18 and 19. The question is, however, whether they are nothing more than the interpolations of a glossator or whether they are an integral, functional part of the narration. Taken in isolation, the phenomenon can certainly be more easily explained as belonging to the former category. If treated in conjunction with several analogous instances, the alternative hypothesis would be favored.[14]

In Gen 22:20-24 a genealogy appears wedged between two momentous events, the Akedah and the purchase of the Cave of Machpelah. It seems to have absolutely no connection with either, and certainly it does not forge a link between them. Yet a close look reveals several instructive features. The genealogy presumes a knowledge of 11:29, which mentions Milcah together with Sarai. The phrase "Milcah too has borne children to your brother Nahor" (22:20) is intelligible only in light of that passage and of the birth of Isaac. At the same time, it explains why Milcah was not described as barren in the earlier listing even though no offspring of hers was recorded there. Whoever inserted the genealogy of 11:29 deliberately withheld the list of her children because it has a special function in 22:20ff. The remarks relating to "Kemuel the father of Aram" and "Bethuel being the father of Rebekah" are clues to the function of the genealogy and point to the reason for its presence here. The previous pericope closed with divine blessings, and for these to be fulfilled Isaac must marry and found a family. The list therefore mentions Rebekah, Bethuel, Milcah, Nahor, and Aram as an intimation of Isaac's forthcoming marriage to Rebekah daughter of Bethuel son of Milcah of the city of Nahor in Aram-naharaim. In this way, its presence after the Akedah is purposeful, anticipating the events of ch. 24.

That chapter, too, contains elements that exemplify this narrative technique of slipping in seemingly innocent phrases that are portentous of later developments. The opening sentence reads as follows: "Abraham was now old, advanced in years, and the LORD had blessed Abraham in all things." This final clause appears to have no particular relevance to the matter at hand, which is the finding of a wife for the forty-year-old bachelor Isaac. Since it is the patriarch's extreme old age that lends urgency to the quest, the note about God's blessing of Abraham actually disturbs the smooth flow of the narration. It soon becomes clear, however, that Abraham's material wealth is crucial to the matchmaking procedure. The servant sets out with an entourage of ten camels carrying "all the bounty of his master" (v 10). He presents the girl who waters his beasts with expensive gold jewelry (v 22), and she and her family receive gifts of silver and gold, of garments and other things, once the negotiations are brought to a successful conclusion (v 53). Furthermore, the servant cleverly stresses his master's great wealth in his ad-

14. Cf. J. Skinner, *Genesis*, International Critical Commentary, 2nd ed. (New York, 1930): "This notice of the sinfulness of Sodom is another anticipation of ch. 19."

dress to the bride's family: "The LORD has greatly blessed my master, and he has given him sheep and cattle, silver and gold, male and female slaves, camels and asses" (v 35). All this is critical to the softening-up process for the difficult task of persuading the girl and her family to consent to the marriage and to agree to her leaving home for travel to a distant land. The ultimate inducement is, of course, the servant's declaration that Isaac is Abraham's sole heir (v 36). Seen in the light of all these facts, the apparently intrusive opening remark about God having "blessed Abraham in all things" becomes endowed with literary importance and latent meaning. The same applies to the statement that "Rebekah had a brother whose name was Laban" and that when he saw the golden nose-ring and bracelets he "ran out to the man at the spring" (vv 29–30). Can it be doubted that here is an insight into Laban's character intended to prepare the reader for the developments of chs. 29–31?

The story of the birth of Rebekah's twins, Esau and Jacob, and of their rivalry for the birthright is replete with anticipatory data. We are informed of the elder son's red complexion[15] and hirsute body (25:25). Neither detail is again mentioned in the immediately ensuing narrative. It is clear, however, that the two descriptions provide etiologies for the names Edom and Seir, with both of which Esau is explicitly identified later in Genesis.[16] At the same time, the hairiness of Esau turns out to be crucial to the events of the next episode.[17] The same is true of Esau's being "a skillful hunter" (v 27) and of Isaac's fondness for game, a weakness that led him to favor Esau over Jacob (v 28). Every one of these facts is indispensable to the understanding of how Jacob succeeded in extracting the birthright blessing from his father by means of trickery (ch. 27).

Chapter 26 is the one section wholly concerned with Isaac. All other traditions relating to this patriarch are integrated into the biographies of Abraham or Jacob. In the account of the sundry adventures preserved in this chapter, there is not a hint of Isaac's being a family man. The two sons do not figure in any way in the various incidents, which, in fact, may well have taken place before their birth.[18] Yet, suddenly, the chapter ends with a remark about Esau's Hittite wives, who are a source of bitterness and vexation to his parents (vv 34–35). This extraordinary addendum, totally unrelated to what precedes, must either be a clumsy interpolation or else, on the contrary, its very discontinuity and irregularity belong to the rhetorical strategies of a gifted writer and constitute an important element of the creative process. Now, the perceptive reader will doubtless observe at once that the intrusive nature of Esau's marital affairs recalls the place and role of the genealogies of 11:10–32 and 22:20–24, both of which appear to be contextually extraneous but turn out to afford essential data preparatory to subsequent narrative developments. In like manner, the remarks presently under discussion make Rebekah's complaint to her husband in 27:46 intelligible. Having been apprised of Esau's

15. *Contra* Th. H. Gaster, *Myth, Legend and Custom in the O.T.* (New York, 1975), I, pp. 164f., this is more likely to be the meaning of *ʾdmwny* than is "redheadedness," if only for the reason that the latter's folkloristic association with the sinister and the dangerous is inappropriate to David, who is also, and approvingly, described as being *ʾdmwny* (1 Sam 16:12; 17:14). For a possible explanation of the ruddy complexion, see C. H. Gordon, *The Ancient Near East*, 3rd. rev. ed. (New York, 1965), p. 125 n. 26.

16. Esau is identified with Edom in 36:1, 8, 19; cf. vv 9, 43. Seir is the homeland of Esau in 33:14, 16; 36:8f., 21; Deut 2:4, 5, 8, 12, 22, 29; Josh 24:4.

17. Gen 27:11, 16, 23.

18. H. Hupfeld, *Die Quellen der Genesis* (Berlin, 1853), p. 155; cf. S. D. Luzzatto, *Commentary to the Pentateuch*, ed. P. Schlesinger (Tel-Aviv, 1965), p. 107.

murderous threat against Jacob, she realizes that, for his own safety, her younger son must be sent away (42-48). But she cannot disclose to her husband the true reason for Jacob's impending departure, and so she hits upon the pretext that it is time for the boy to marry. " 'I am disgusted with my life because of the Hittite women,' " she says to Isaac. " 'If Jacob marries a Hittite woman like these, from among the native women, what good will life be to me?' " The persuasiveness of this argument is decisive because, as 26:34-35 have already informed us, Esau's union with the local women has already turned out to be an intolerable torment to Isaac, and so he readily grants his consent (28:1-2).

My last example of the sort of device that I am illustrating here is 35:22. We are told that "While Israel stayed in that land, Reuben went and lay with Bilhah, his father's concubine; and Israel found out." The disagreeable details that form the background to this strange interlude have obviously been suppressed,[19] but a little light on this truncated story is shed by the Chronicler:

> The sons of Reuben the firstborn of Israel—for he was the firstborn; but when he disgraced his father's bed, his rank of firstborn was given to the sons of Joseph son of Israel, so he is not reckoned as firstborn in the genealogy.
> (1 Chron 5:1)

The Chronicler was certainly aware of much more than tradition has transmitted in Gen 35:22. What is particularly puzzling about the latter passage is the final phrase, which literally means "and Jacob heard," for the sentence is complete without it. Possessing no direct object, and indicating no reaction on Jacob's part, it juts out as a literary *membrum suspensum*, and one wonders why it is there. The most plausible solution is that suggested by Rashbam, who refers to Gen 49:3f. In his deathbed testament, Jacob condemns Reuben for his immoral act: "For when you mounted your father's bed, you brought disgrace." Because of it, Reuben forfeited his birthright. Brief and obscure though it be, the note of 35:22, which tells of the incident and informs us that Jacob heard about it even though he did not witness it, saves the poetic passage of 49:3f. from unintelligibility.

Gerhard von Rad has rightly pointed out that, in dealing with the individual units of the Book of Genesis, "one must not lose sight of the great unit of which they are but parts," and that in its present form, it is "the narrative as a whole and the contexts into which all the individual parts fit and from which they are to be understood"[20] that must be kept in mind. The literary feature demonstrated above crosses all conventional source-critical divisions.[21] For this reason, it deserves to be taken seriously in any examination of the literary structure and ultimate unity of the Book of Genesis.

19. In the received Hebrew text, a *pisqaʾ beʾemṣaʿ pasuq* appears after *yiśrāʾēl*, indicating some anomaly. For a comprehensive review of the research on this scribal phenomenon, see P. Sandler, in *D. Neiger Volume* (Jerusalem, 1959), pp. 222-48, to which should be added Sh. Talmon, *Textus*, V (1966), pp. 14-20.

20. *Genesis*, p. 13.

21. Thus, 9:18, 22 are assigned to J, but 10:6 to P; 11:10-26 are ascribed to P, vv 27-32 to P and J, vv 28-30 to J, 28b to JE, and 12:1-8 to Jh, but ch. 24 goes to J, 29:5 to J or JE, 31:53 to E or JE, and 20:12 to E; 13:10, 14, and chs. 18 and 19 are attributed to J, with a dash of P in 19; 11:29; 22:20-24, and ch. 24 are all credited to J; 25:15 is linked to P, but vv 27, 28 to J, while ch. 27 is accounted to J or JE; 26:34f., 27:46, and 28:1-2 are all consistently assigned to P; finally, 35:22 is ascribed to J, but 45:3-4 are regarded as problematic.

CONCLUSION

Radical Editing
Redaktionsgeschichte and the Aesthetic
of Willed Confusion*

JOHN RUSSIANO MILES

I write as a former Bible scholar, at least a formerly aspiring Bible scholar, who has now become an editor. But if all Bible scholars, to the extent that they are preoccupied with redaction, must become editors, then I hope I may still have something in common with my former colleagues. In the course of this paper, I hope to compare ancient and modern editing and to ask whether the difference between them makes any difference for contemporary Bible interpretation. I think it does.

By answering this question, however, I hope to get at a larger question. Why has criticism of other literatures had so slight an impact on the criticism of the Bible as literature? It has not been so for the study of the Bible as history or as religion or as folklore. It has not been so for the many ancillary disciplines: philology, linguistics, archaeology, etc. In the latter, borrowing has been the rule, not the exception. But I think few will quarrel with my assertion that borrowing from other literary studies has been exceptional in Bible studies. Why so? What has got in the way?

In the body of this paper I shall argue two theses that may answer that question. My first thesis, which looks backward, is that modern Bible critics, whether Christians, Jews, or unbelievers, have shared a quasi-religious commitment to history. Their belief in the possibility of rendering the Bible historically coherent has seemed distinct from and, privately, often more important than their commitment to any traditional creed. In any event, that belief has been only part of their belief in the larger possibility of rendering an historically coherent account of all reality. I am not aware that any historian has said of history what I. A. Richards in a weak moment said of poetry, namely, that it can "save us." But I submit that something more has been at stake for historians, most particularly for Bible historians, than learning from the past so as not to repeat its mistakes.

If history and literature have been rivals for the privilege of saving us, then it is plain with which of the rivals Bible scholarship has cast its lot. Bible scholarship as taught and practiced in the best American universities has not been skeptical, much less derisive, about the possibility and value of history, and so it has found the mood of modern literature—and, by derivation, the mood of modern literary theory—which is, indeed, skeptical and sometimes derisive about history, to be most unlike its own mood.

---

*An earlier version of this paper appeared in *Traditions in Transformation: Turning-Points in Biblical Faith*, Frank Moore Cross *Festschrift*, B. Halpern and J. Levenson, eds., published by Eisenbrauns (Winona Lake, Indiana, 1981).

My second thesis, which looks forward, is that as this mood now shifts, as interest in history and skepticism about literary studies give way to skepticism about history and interest in literary studies, as Bible critics, in short, begin to apostatize from history as a quasi-religion, they may appropriate for their own purposes an aesthetic well-established in poetry and fiction. I call the latter the aesthetic of willed confusion.

Let us turn now to the promised consideration of ancient and modern editing and see whether and how we may be led thence to the conclusions just stated.

The Bible is arguably unique among the world's religious literatures for the self-consciousness that it displays vis-à-vis editorial processes and their importance. Later Jewish tradition has tended to conceal the Hebrew plural *tôrāh nᵊbîʾîm ukᵊtûbîm* ("Law, Prophets, and Writings") beneath the opaque acronym *tanakh* ("Laprow"). Western Christian tradition has lost the Greek plural *biblia* ("Books") in the Latin singular *Scriptura* and vernacular singulars like the English *Bible*. But against this tendency, the separate attributions of separate books within the Bible have not been suppressed; moreover, within a single book—the Book of Psalms, for instance—there may be indications of significantly varying social contexts. Modern scholarship may challenge attributions, make further separations within books traditionally regarded as units, and further specify the contexts. We should bear in mind, however, that the recognition of division and subdivision within the collection was as strong at the beginning as it is now and has survived all efforts at forced harmonization.

In short, a concern with editorial questions of the sort that turn the Good Book into a shelf of books whose goodness varies is not fundamentally alien to the tradition that wrote and has continued to read the Bible. Particular editorial answers may be rejected, but editorial questions are as scriptural as Scripture itself. The very rationalist spirit of modern scholarship has its antecedents in the biblical text to the extent that the multiplication of attributions, glosses, and the like bespeaks a determination that the real raggedness of the collection not disappear wholly into the seamless unity of God. A truly sacralized, hypostatized text, a text turned into a fetish or an idol, could risk no such specificity about its origins. It would have to be—as so many myths are—anonymous and undated. The identification of so many biblical authors has offered critics—not just in modern times but from the beginning—that many opportunities and more to ask the questions that keep the genealogy of the Bible in view. It is not true, therefore, that the King James Version of the Bible is the only masterpiece ever produced by a committee. The Bible itself is such a masterpiece, a masterpiece of editing that has paraded its editing almost from the start.

In its analysis of editing, its *Redaktionsgeschichte*, contemporary Bible criticism usually assumes the universality of the classical principle *Ars est celare artem*, "Art is the hiding of art." The ancient editors of the biblical texts are assumed to intend—as the editors of a modern work would intend—to conceal their editorial handiwork as much as possible. A work attributed to one man should be made to read as the work of one man. A work purporting to deal with only one subject should be made to deal with that subject alone. A work dealing with times and places should be kept coherent as to chronology and geography. When it is not so, contemporary critics commonly "detect" an inconsistent editorial hand, the implication being that what has now been discovered was not intended for discovery.

Now, I concede that some of the editorial work in the Bible was not intended for discovery. I would point out, however, that the Bible may be most striking among ancient religious writings not for the editorial information it withholds but for the editorial information it provides. If the biblical editors knew so well how to provide information when they chose to, then when they do not, we should not assume that the cause is simple carelessness. It may rather be the operation of another aesthetic principle than *Ars est celare artem*. What is this principle?

Often, the impression the biblical text gives is that of incomplete editing. When two accounts of one event are included, there will often, yes, be an attempt at harmonization, an indication that someone, some editor, was indeed aware that the presence of two accounts constituted a problem. But the harmonization is rarely thoroughgoing. (I say "rarely" because, obviously, when it *is* thoroughgoing we do not know about it.) It was this sense of incomplete or interrupted editing that led the late William Foxwell Albright to characterize ancient Israelite society as "proto-logical," taking that term to be a midpoint between "pre-logical" and "logical." Ancient Israelite society was neither happily primitive, wholly undisturbed about logical matters, nor yet as careful about them as the Greeks would be and as we are. If the Greek invention of logic was a revolution, then, as Albright saw it, ancient Israel, meaning a culture whose continuity was not broken until A.D. 135, was in a restive, pre-revolutionary state of mind. Our question must be: what aesthetic, if any, was proper to that state of mind?

When a contemporary critic comes across an original composition reflecting a plainly primitive mentality, he is quite content to leave it alone. Indeed, such compositions have their deepest appeal in our day precisely by virtue of their distance from logic. But primitive *editing*—or, much worse, half-primitive, half-sophisticated editing—is less respectfully dealt with. Of an editor, even an ancient editor, the modern sensibility demands logic, precisely so that the absence of logic may shine forth at the appropriate moment. There is a chamber of unreason within the modern mind, and the portal opening upon it bears the warning: "Let him who is without logic *and him only* enter here." Accordingly, when a logical mind observes a style of editing that mars a pre-logical literary effect on what may now appear poorly conceived or badly implemented logical grounds, the logical mind is offended and wants to step in. In effect, the contemporary, fully logical critic wants to defend the ancient, pre-logical writer against the bad taste of the ancient, partially logical editor.

Until now, Bible criticism has not produced an edition of the Bible purporting to correct all the errors of this order that Bible critics claim to have detected in the work of the ancient Israelite editors. Annotations pointing out the errors, yes, but corrected editions, no. But times may be changing. Doubleday has just published Stephen Mitchell's *Into the Whirlwind*, a translation of the Book of Job from which an ancient editor's addition, the speeches of Elihu, has been excised. The first author, or at least an earlier editor, doubtless intended us to hear the first words of God in ch. 38 directly after the last words of Job in ch. 31. The effect of reading the text in this way is undeniably powerful. But by what right, many would ask, does this modern translator tamper so drastically with a text hallowed by history and by religious tradition? Can he really call such a tampering a translation at all? Is it not, rather, a selection from the Book of Job, or at most a condensation of the Book of Job? The answer, I submit, is that *Into the Whirlwind* is, in the unapologetic contemporary sense, an edition of the Book of Job.

Historical critics of the Bible should not be surprised to see their work used as Mitchell has used it. It is of the essence of critical Bible scholarship to seek to discern a better Bible within the received Bible. Critical commentaries—as they analyze the accidents of physical transmission and seek to undo the effects of cultural oblivion—are all in effect memos to some future, bolder scholar-editor, explaining to him what a true edition of the Bible would require, what portion of the original text he should put in footnotes, what in an appendix, what in the margin, etc., and what, perhaps, he should set in bold type with a dateline as the reconstituted original.

A few years ago, a well-regarded British scholar, Joseph Rhymer, published a translation with commentary entitled *The Bible in Order*, suggesting, plainly enough, that what we had all been reading was the Bible out of order. James Charlesworth, director of the Duke University pseudepigrapha project, has suggested publicly that the canon be revised to include some of the writings his group studies. Written by Jews, preserved by Christians, some of the pseudepigrapha, Charles would maintain, are intrinsically worthy of as much respect as the canonized writings that antedate and postdate them.

If I may digress for just a moment on the subject of the Bible canon, I would point out that there are currently at least four canons in use. The Samaritans reject what the Jews added, the Samaritans and Jews reject what the Christians added, and the Catholics retain what the Protestants subtracted. It is hardly to be ruled out in principle that some further revision in one or more of these canons could take place. The Samaritans could admit the Jewish prophets as apocrypha. The Protestants could admit the present Apocrypha as Scripture. The Jews could canonize the *Pirke Abot*. Catholics and Protestants together could de-canonize the Pastoral Letters. To borrow a popular expression that seems quaintly appropriate, the canon as canon is not written in stone.

And let us bear in mind that no less than the redaction of any individual biblical book, the question of the Bible canon as a whole is an editorial question. The layman thinks of the professional editor principally in his involvement with the revision of manuscripts, but revision is a second stage. The first stage is acceptance or rejection. Each editor in a book-publishing company has his own list—his canon, if you will—which he compiles according to criteria that are usually intuitive and certainly never publicized as such. Though no editor troubles to do it, any editor could compile a list of noteworthy rejected books, a secular *Tosefta* of works unpublished or, if published, judged unworthy of a given imprint. Be that as it may, rivalry can arise between the ancient and modern editor over the canon as a whole as easily as it does over the redaction of a given book. If the modern editor can produce a better canon than the ancient editors did, why should he not do so?

Three reactions to the prospect of such radical editing are both possible and coherent. First, one may simply endorse it, as if to say, "This is just the kind of scholarship we need. Now at last we shall see what the intentions of the biblical authors really were." A second reaction is to endorse radical editing only as a stage. Such editing may show us the intentions of the biblical authors as separate agents, but a further act of criticism, it is confidently believed, will show us the intentions of the editors who created the collection as a collection. This I take to be the intent and the hope of *Redaktionsgeschichte*. A third reaction is to reject radical editing as theoretically possible but out of keeping with the general mission of Bible criticism, namely, that of preserving and promoting the Bible in the form in which it has actually been operative in Western religious and cultural history.

The last reaction, though coherent, is in context an evasion of responsibility. The entire thrust of critical Bible scholarship has been author-based, not reader-based. Religiously orthodox criticism has been, by intent at least, supremely author-based, studying the Bible as the Word of God, not as a mere artifact in the ongoing life of a human community. One may, of course, take the role of the Bible as canonized and influential over time for the object of one's study, but such study is not Bible criticism, strictly speaking, however appealing it may be.

By contrast, the first reaction of the three, that which would simply endorse radical editing, is a good deal more responsible. Radical editing does stand in direct continuity with all that has been most active and most serious in critical scholarship. There can be and possibly will be a good deal more of it than we have seen. The suggestion in it that the leap to *Redaktionsgeschichte* has been hasty may well be a good one. The shocking implications of historical criticism have probably not yet been adequately tasted. We have not yet gazed long enough on the peculiar new Bible that a legion of scholars, each re-constructing a separate portion of the text, have written for us. Radical editing may make that contemplation possible to the enrichment of later criticism. And yet there is an evasion in radical editing too. The ancient editors, particularly the very last editors, who created the collection as a collection, are not to be simply ignored. Responsible criticism must at least ask why those editors included so much that radical editing in our day would drop out.

To ask that question is, of course, to choose the second alternative, *Redaktionsgeschichte*, but let us not minimize the difficulty of this alternative. In reconstructing early stages in the history of a text that has gone through many editings, the critic may always blame confusion on some later stage, some later editorial hand. But when the very last stage is reached, the remaining confusion must be dealt with directly. Did the last editor simply do his work badly? If so, then radical editing is vindicated as we find that there is a final stage but one that has added nothing but only detracted. Or has the last editor somehow embraced confusion as an aesthetic principle in itself? I shall argue below that the literary experience of our own day should teach us that confusion can be artistically willed. But if the last editors of the Bible were operating on such a principle, if the proto-logical aesthetic allows for willed confusion, the practical consequences for interpretation are considerable. To begin with, how, at such a cultural remove, is the modern interpreter to distinguish artistically willed confusion from mere ignorance or carelessness? If he can do so at all, he surely cannot do so easily. More challenging still, if an artistically willed confusion characterized the last stage, may it not have characterized some earlier stage as well? If so, then *Redaktionsgeschichte* is possible only via a painstaking reexamination of the putatively assured results of all earlier historical criticism.

Of the aesthetic of willed confusion we shall have more to say later, but that aesthetic is surely familiar enough to require little introduction. It is trite as primitive art in a skyscraper office or a collage of magazine photographs in a high-school student's room, as familiar as rapid cutting during the opening seconds of a television police drama or the newscast that gradually drowns out Paul Simon's voice in his recorded version of "Silent Night." The question we must ask is not whether such an aesthetic is possible but why it seems never to have occurred to Bible critics to seek some variant of it in the Bible. Was this a rational conclusion that no such modern aesthetic could operate in an ancient text? I think not.

It was, rather, the effect of the allegiance of several generations of scholars to history against the claims of religion. The most recent generation of Bible scholars, trained in historical criticism, seems obscurely to know that the fight for the legitimacy of historical against theological criticism has been won. An earlier generation may have had to be alert against the intrusion of theological concerns into historical debate. Today, a more common objection is against the intrusion of prosaic historical concerns into literary appreciation. Or, if it is too much to speak of intrusion, historical criticism is faulted for its lack of eloquence, an invincible blandness in speaking of the literary beauty of Scripture, or the literary quality of it, beautiful or not. The standard works of historical scholarship now seem halting and crude in a literary sense, contented with generalities that their authors would never countenance in linguistic or historical analysis. Diachronic, historical criticism was to have been a *mise-en-scène* for synchronic, literary appreciation. But the *mise-en-scène* seems to have become the performance. Why? And what is to be done?

The notion, sometimes bruited about, of breaking altogether with historical criticism and reading the Bible with fresh literary (or psychological or anthropological) eyes is naïveté of the worst kind. However, the present state of Bible scholarship may well call for a patient *ad hominem* examination to see whether historical scholars' long struggle with authoritative, even authoritarian, religious interpretation has not left them with attitudes that block or slow literary appreciation. History may have had to become religion to resist religion. If historical critics now abandon their larger ambitions, their solemn responsibilities, then they may perceive a chaos in the Bible that they would once have resisted perceiving. With smaller responsibilities, in other words, Bible scholars may be free to take larger risks. If they do and as they do, the large achievement of a century of coherently pursued Bible scholarship may be further enlarged with what has been most authentically prophetic in the poetry and fiction of our own day.

From the point of view of the religious authorities from whom modern historical critics received the "received text," some of the most famous modern scholars have been outright apostates. One thinks, among Christian exegetes, of the vilified David Friedrich Strauss, and of, two generations later, the celebrated Albert Schweitzer. But apostasy, it must be borne in mind, is a religious vocation of a sort. The Christian church has understood itself to be Christian by its careful preservation of certain memories. In some sense, then, those among the Christians who have been most Christian have been those who were most directly charged with deciding what to remember and what to forget. And as these were editorial decisions, we may say that the text of Scripture and its editors or students have consecrated one another reciprocally. The original editors, by their actions of redaction, exclusion, inclusion, etc., consecrated the text. But thereafter, they—and still more their followers—remained holy by association with the holy text. An apostate critic—a Strauss, a Schweitzer—by bringing a new set of criteria for redaction made by implication a new selection among the memories and provided a new and distinct impulse toward religious community. Some modern historical critics have embraced this vocation freely, others greedily; still others have had it thrust upon them, administering a revelation in spite of themselves. But in the religious context in which they began their work, all have been affected to some extent by this inherent power in their work. As in the Old Testament itself, it is sometimes the unwilling prophet who has the inescapable vocation.

Pre-modern Judaism and pre-modern Christianity were concerned with the future.

However, neither thought that the essential truths of human living were still to be revealed, much less that they were still to be constructed. Though Christianity did intend to revise Judaism, it did not intend to introduce revision itself as a principle. It understood God to have offered mankind a new covenant revising the old covenant with the Jews; but it did not expect its own new covenant to become obsolete in its turn. Herbert N. Schneidau, in a remarkable work entitled *Sacred Discontent* (Baton Rouge, Louisiana, 1977), does maintain that the principle of endless revision is at the heart of the tradition that began at the burning bush. This principle explains, he says, why Israel begat a Catholic Church, why the Catholic Church begat a Protestantism, Protestantism an Enlightenment, and the Enlightenment a cultural pluralism that so stimulates and exhausts us. Whether or not Schneidau is correct, it certainly is *not* the case that either Judaism or Christianity has publicly celebrated the joy of revision. Both have endured revision, all right; but only in rationalism is revision made something like a sacred principle in its own right.

Now, as regards revision, there is a real difference between a Jewish exegete who wants to be a new Rashi, even if he uses modern methods, and one who wants to be a new Moses, just as there is a difference between a Christian exegete who wants to be a new Luther and one who wants to be a new Christ. This difference is the difference between traditional exegesis, beholden to a community and opposed in principle to revision, and non-traditional exegesis, beholden to no community and in favor only of the paradoxical principle of continuous revision. Any philosophical arguments that can be adduced for traditional rabbinic exegesis, beholden to the Jewish community, are likely to serve equally well as arguments for traditional ecclesiastical exegesis, beholden to the Christian church. Luther is the same sort of boast and the same sort of embarrassment to the Lutheran that Rashi is to the Jew. A Jewish scholar who wants to study anthropology, archaeology, and other modern disciplines without abandoning Rashi is very like a Christian scholar who might want to study the same disciplines without abandoning Luther. But is such an enterprise in double citizenship possible?

It may be well to ask at this point just what a religiously motivated exegete is likely to end up doing if he undertakes critical biblical scholarship. I submit that he is likely to end up writing history—and offering his work as a modest contribution to that comprehensive account of reality from its beginning to its end, from its top to its bottom, that history in our day intends to be. The British philosopher R. G. Collingwood, author of both *The Idea of Nature* and *The Idea of History*, regarded our Western idea of history as finally including our idea of nature. Nature, as we know now, is not constant. An astrophysicist like Lloyd Motz, author of *The Universe: Its Beginning and Its End*, can provide you with the history of a single element; he can tell you when and under what circumstances the element iron first appeared in the universe and when and under what circumstances it will disappear. Relative to the quick changes of a love affair, iron seems durable, but it is not immutable: it has a life cycle of a sort. Motz reports that the very scientific laws operative since the Big Bang and until the collapse of matter may obtain only for that interval; i.e., after the next Big Bang, if there is one, there may be an entirely new set of scientific laws. Of such changes the only sense that can be made is not scientific but historical. The idea of history, then, as including all conceivable changes and charting all provisional stabilities for as long as they obtain, is our largest, most inclusive idea. As such it is nothing less than an alternative revelation.

Perceiving it as that, we can appreciate the difficulty that faces an exegete who would amend the Bible text for religious motives but by historical methods; viz., if history taken as a whole is an alternative revelation, then when an editor uses the methods of the historian to improve the Bible, he corrects one revelation by the methods of another. One need not deny that his correction is possible or even, subjectively, a devout act. One must insist, however, that the religion it serves is not the religion that the original editors served. Those ancient editors saw no larger context into which the Bible could be inserted. The context that, by stages, the biblical writers created—the context that stretched in time from the first day of creation to the Day of the Lord and in space from Jerusalem outward to the Nations—was, literally, the largest context they could imagine. It was the cosmos. To create a larger context would have been then, as it is now, to found a new religion, or at least to challenge, radically, the adequacy of the old. It would be to consecrate a new clerisy of history holy in a new reciprocal relationship with the emerging sacred text of universal history itself. A critic who wished to take his stand with the old clerisy rather than the new might well decline, for that reason, to deal too critically with the text. Pre-critical exegesis has survived and will survive; on its own ground, it has not been defeated by critical exegesis. However, even on its own ground, its self-awareness has been modified by the silent presence of an alternative. Even where it is authoritative still, it exercises its authority in a new way.

But how authoritative, for those who know it best, is this new alternative? I submit that the authority of the historical criticism of the Bible can be no stronger than the authority of history itself in the broadest sense and that history in just that sense, i.e., as a comprehensive, organizing discipline, a field of fields, marshaling the forces of learning, is in trouble. The more Bible critics are skeptical about history, the less aggressively they will be inclined to use the tools that historical criticism has placed at their disposal. I sense that many Bible critics are indeed increasingly skeptical about history, not because of shortcomings in Bible historians themselves but because of what I can only call a mood swing in higher learning. This mood swing affects all higher learning, but particularly those fields that are, like history, highly synthetic.

In the recent past, the metaphor that best caught the mood of learning was that of *avant-garde*: a metaphor of direction, landscape, compass, and armies on the march. A far more appropriate and, appropriately, a far more common metaphor today is that of *wavelength*: a metaphor of signal and interference that we hear in such American slang as *tuned in*, *tuned out*, *turned on*, *static*, *vibrations*, and *on my wavelength*. A given signal plays my whole radio so long as I tune to that signal. Different signals, while simultaneously possible, for me are not complementary but mutually exclusive. When the organizing metaphor was military and geographic, several avant-gardes could be wonderfully visible to one another: there could be and there were avant-garde art, avant-garde poetry, avant-garde politics, avant-garde child-rearing—all part of the same brave vanguard advancing across the same terrain toward the same retreating enemy. But different frequencies on my FM dial do not relate the way different battalions did in that advancing army. The different battalions of an avant-garde remain elaborately, urgently in touch. Radio stations on different wavelengths act as if each were the only station on the air.

The difference between these two metaphors, I think, points up a crucial skepticism in contemporary thought, a defeated privatization that now affects Bible scholars' confidence in historical criticism. This mood of privatization, I hasten to add, has not been created by radio or TV. Radio as a medium may have its own message. I speak of radio only as a metaphor for a message. For a fuller statement of the same message, I turn to a student of communications theory, Michel Serre.

In his provocative book *Interférence*, this French thinker has written: "We must read interference as inter-reference" (p. 15). But Serre is ironic: he knows that one must also read inter-reference as outright interference, as static. Interdisciplinary cooperation is mutual obstruction pursued to strained smiles at best. By what intellectual right does any intellectual presume to *situate* another intellectual's work within his own intellectual synthesis! *Situation* bespeaks compass and terrain, but that is the language of the past. One cannot situate one frequency on another frequency. Simultaneously valid, the two are mutually exclusive. Serre writes:

> Il n'y aurait pas de science-reine, de théorie des théories en référence à quoi le savoir, dans sa totalité mouvante, dessinerait son arborescence: et comme reine, et comme science. Qui parle bien de l'ordre est dans l'ordre, ou son langage est mal formé; la science des sciences est l'une d'elles—génitif partitif—ou elle n'est pas science. Une politique. (p. 20)

> There is no queen science, no theory of theories in relation to which knowing, in its ongoing totality, would work out its ramifications both as queen and as science. You cannot speak of order without being in the order of which you speak, anything else is misuse of language. The science of sciences is one *of* the sciences—the genitive is partitive—or it is not a science, but only politics.

That there is no *science des sciences* but only a kind of politics is another way of announcing the collapse of the nineteenth-century, Hegelian ideal of universal history. The great systematic thinkers of the nineteenth century—Conte, Hegel, Dilthey—did believe that the various disciplines could be assigned their proper places in a common intellectual undertaking. Theology had once been the queen of the sciences, philosophy the *ancilla*, the handmaiden. When philosophy became queen, it was as philosophy of history. Serre describes our day as one in which the proliferation of autonomous scientific and humanistic disciplines has led to the abolition of monarchy itself, as if to cry, "History is dead."

But with the failure of history as universal arbiter, who *is* to mediate conflicting claims among disciplines? Within each discipline, there are those who entertain—as reactionaries, as crypto-monarchists—illicit ambitions. Who is to restrain them? Linguists conquer history by studying the language of history. Historians conquer language by studying the history of linguistics. Philosophers study fiction as philosophy. English professors study philosophers as writers. And so it goes. Whose discipline is properly regarded as most inclusive? The absence of any agreed-upon answer to that question is the determining condition of all thought in our day, as of all thoughtful art, and finally of all Bible criticism as well. History is no longer the study to which the various specializations within Bible scholarship all eventually contribute. History is no longer the discipline of choice for an aspiring student of the Bible. There is no discipline of choice, for there is no basis on which to choose. The choice of research paradigm is a matter of faith or whim or, as Serre would have it, of politics.

I submit that, consciously or unconsciously, most Bible scholars have made crucial professional choices for no compelling intellectual reasons. This is not to fault them. Why should they be the exception to so general a rule? The question to ask about them is *ad hominem*; namely, as they grow aware of the arbitrary in their professional, intellectual lives, what is it about the Bible that they are most likely to notice? I answer: they are likely to see the arbitrary in it, the fragmentary, the contradictory, the accidental, and the stylistically ill-assorted. I suggest: in some ironic way the Bible scholarship of the future is likely to celebrate these erstwhile embarrassments.

Why? Well, why is it that poet-prophets of our era like Ezra Pound have been so drawn to the fragmentary and the unfinished in art and to the juxtaposition in language of past and present, high culture and low, sacred and profane? In a remarkable bit of literary sleuthing, Hugh Kenner explains one example of this fascination in Pound as follows (5-6):

> What Sappho conceived on one occasion on Mitylene is gone beyond reconstitution; the sole proof that she ever conceived it is a scrap from a parchment copy made thirteen centuries later on; on an upper left-hand corner learning assisted by chemicals makes out a few letters; in *Berliner Klassikertexte*, V-2, 1907, pp. 14-15, type stands for those letters with perhaps misleading decisiveness:
>
> .Ρ’Α[. . .
> ΔΗΡΑΤ.[. . .
> ΓΟΓΓΥΛΑ.[. . .
>
> . . . plus the beginnings of perhaps a dozen more lines: very possibly, so modern editions indicate, the first aorist of the verb *to raise* (conjecturing ἦρά), and a word unknown, and the name of a girl of Sappho's. Or you can remember from Alcaeus and Ibycus ἦρ, the contraction for *springtime*, and derive the unknown word from δηρός, *too long*, and write
>
> Spring . . . .
> Too long . . . .
> Gongula . . . .
>
> heading the little witticism "Papyrus" and printing it in a book of poems called *Lustra* as an exemplum for resurrection-men. And wait decades for someone to unriddle it.

Why did Pound write this cryptic poem? Why, having written it, did he not at least entitle it "After a fragment in the *Berliner Klassike Texte*"? Was it really intended only for Kenner or a reader like him? I think not: I think it was intended equally for all of us, for all the readers who would *not* understand it. It was given no more informative title because the author did not wish to inform more than he did. And why did he write it in the first place? Is the world not full enough of fragmentation and misinformation and half-truth and puzzlement already? Why add wantonly to the confusion?

The reason why, I think, is that when we are bold enough to create confusion for our own pleasure, we tell ourselves that the confusion inflicted upon us by circumstance is bearable and even enjoyable. We tell ourselves that we can defeat it, that we are as tough as it is, that it doesn't scare us much. After long labors at beating chaos by drawing order from it, we collapse in exhaustion and then, for the first time, see a way to beat chaos by embracing a disorderly beauty within it and creating a manageable, pet chaos of our own. Pound's poem may have many meanings or none.

Though redaction criticism has arisen within the historical criticism of the Bible, its implication is that at times the Bible too may have many meanings or none. The earlier techniques of Bible criticism—source criticism, form criticism, tradition criticism, etc.—were relentlessly preoccupied with the author and the coherence of his vision. The author was often anonymous and had to be named after the text he had written. The critic was, nevertheless, intensely involved with the author and had implicit faith in his rationality. Poor man, his work may have suffered at the hands of copyists. It may have been distorted by the addition of material that conflicted factually with his own. It may have been stylistically modernized or archaized, added to, subtracted from, violated in a hundred ways. But a sensitive critic could undo all the damage and permit the ancient author to speak with his own calm ardor. If there were two authors, both voices could be heard. If an intervening, harmonizing author, three voices. If an inhibiting ideology was detectable, that too could be assessed. And redaction criticism ultimately could isolate the elusive point of view—the editorial intent—of the last mind to have shaped the work before its transmission became a matter of copying. But in the search for this last elusive working, I submit that the reasonability of historical criticism as a whole has to be reappraised.

It must be so because, as noted earlier, when the last redaction is reached there is no longer any later editor on whom to blame remaining inconsistencies. The redactor may seem to be motivated by a concern for surface smoothness in conflated texts—but only sometimes: sometimes he cares more about reverence for received accounts, no matter how many or how badly at variance with each other. Or a theological bias may control him—but not at every point. Or a political allegiance—but only residually. When such inconsistency is discovered in a supposed written document or an oral tradition, it can be blamed on the redactor. But if in the end the remaining inconsistencies must be simply accepted as unexplainable, then one must object: why could the same inconsistencies not be accepted on the same basis at some earlier stage?

How odd it is to reflect that during the same decades when American and British Bible scholarship was so determinedly naming the anonymous writers of the Bible, our own vernacular poetry was in headlong pursuit of anonymity. In the "New Criticism," now no longer new, the text was to stand alone, as if authorless, a brute fact of language. If there were abrupt changes of voice or mood in it, these were all part of it and were not to be gainsaid by any reference to an author and his delicate intentions. The appeal that the Bible continued to have for the poets of that generation owed much to the ancient redactors' failure quite to eliminate the rough, the abrupt, the quizzical, the *hapax legomena*, the pointlessly repetitive, the unglossed and unglossable, the impenetrable. And thus the question arises now: if our best poets were so taken with this editorial failure, can we be sure it was a failure?

Owen Barfield has spoken of early man's sense of oneness with the cosmos as "original participation" and of the sense of oneness to which contemporary man may aspire as "final participation." But language is a part of the cosmos, a physical thing of throats and tongues and teeth and tympana. Final participation must include reacquaintance with all that. The shift of attention in recent poetry from poetic intention to verbal fact seems calculated to get this reacquaintance under way. The brain, after all, is a physical thing, and recent writers have listened to their own brains as a man might listen to his own pulse, palpate his eyeballs beneath their lids, or know the noise of his own excretion. We are all familiar, at least by report, with Eastern meditation techniques in which the purposeful, organizing portion of the mind is neutralized by being assigned a topic without content: a nonsense syllable, the sound of one's breathing, or an unanswerable riddle. I submit that the parade of images, memories, etc., that occurs in meditation is a physical, participative experience of the brain. I can touch my hand when I am not using it. This is how I "touch" my brain.

And when a Joyce writes in the stream of consciousness, splicing together passages from crazily assorted sources, it is to this that he invites his readers. This is physical participation in the experience of being an intelligent animal, both intelligent and an animal. But again, ancient texts, notably the Hebrew Bible, often create a similar spliced effect. Doubtless we are right to assume that the ancient author was not striving, as Joyce was, for splicedness as such. But *unconscious does not mean unfelt*. An ancient redactor may not have sought the jarring and the truncated the way some modern poets have, and yet his tolerance of it may have been artistically motivated. That it did not bother him enough for him to eliminate it must mean that, to some extent, he simply liked it. Paul Ricoeur is celebrated for coining the phrases "first naïveté" and "second naïveté" for the interpretation of myth. But for Bible interpretation, I prefer Barfield's "final participation," extended now to cover the primitive flow of the Bible's language and the half-intended disarray of its contents.

The very last thing I want to suggest is that poets are the unacknowledged legislators of the race or that artists are the priests of nature. Artists have a job to do like everybody else. Sometimes changes in mood that eventually will touch everyone actually touch artists last. In this particular case, however, I do believe that modern poets and a few novelists felt first something that contemporary Bible critics are only now about to feel. It is the critics' inability to imagine an aesthetic of disorder, or of deliberately mingled order and disorder, that may separate them most sharply from the ancient writers and editors they study. As they acquire this ability, perhaps by relinquishing what in modern times has been their quasi-religious vocation, they may find that they have less taste for the harmony and smoothness that historical scholarship would impose on the text. This is a matter of taste, but I think it a matter of great consequence, too.

Let me bring this paper to a conclusion by reflecting briefly on a line from Montesquieu which the Catholic theologian Hans Urs von Balthasar invokes in his study of the Protestant theologian Karl Barth. The line is: "The Catholic religion will destroy the Protestant religion, and then Catholics will become Protestants." If by the Catholic religion one understands that form of Christianity that set human authority, the church, over scriptural authority, then it is plain how the Catholic religion has now destroyed the Protestant religion. The Protestant principle of *solā Scripturā*, "by Scripture alone," that led to the modern critical study of Scripture has now concluded that what lies behind the Bible text at every point is not a revelatory event but a believing community. Those ancient editors, those ancient redactors, those ancient canonizers—they were, after all, a very human authority. That the critical methods that sought to exalt Scripture have ended by exalting these editorial nobodies, these ancient anonymities, is in archetypal terms a victory for Catholicism over Protestantism.

Though Montesquieu did not have Bible criticism in mind, I fancy that in his sly, rationalist way he did foresee that the Protestants, however ardent they were in his day, would in the end despair of the attempt to obey God directly and would create an intermediate human authority as cold and scandalous as the papacy. In other words, he saw that rationalism was inevitable in religion and that Catholicism, earlier and more infected with rationalism, was thereby the wave of the future. Matthew Arnold paid the Church of Rome the same oblique compliment in a comment on Pope Pius IX, the nineteenth-century pope whose Vatican Council defined the doctrine of papal infallibility:

> The infallible Church Catholic is, really, the prophetic soul of the wide world dreaming on things to come; the whole race, in its onward progress, developing truth more complete than the parcel of truth any momentary individual can seize. Nay, even that amiable old pessimist in St. Peter's Chair, whose allocutions we read and call them impotent and vain,—the Pope

himself is, in his idea, the very Time-Spirit taking flesh, the incarnate "Zeit-Geist"! O man, how true are thine instincts, how overhasty thine interpretations of them!
Literature and Dogma, An Essay Toward A Better Apprehension of the Bible (Boston, 1873)

Catholicism was an offense to Protestantism because of the way in which the popes seemed to make up their Christianity as they went along, but, obviously, this was no special offense to rationalism, which was convinced in any event that *all* religions were made up by men as they went along. There was, in effect, a pope lurking in the bushes of even the most primal, archetypal religion. There was no escaping him because there was no escaping the scandal of human responsibility for human behavior, even in religion.

Catholicism, I hardly need add, has never laid claim to first honors in acknowledged rationalism. Views tending very delicately in this direction were condemned by Rome in the Modernist controversy at the turn of the nineteenth century. For two generations, every Catholic priest had to take a formal oath against Modernism before his ordination. But centuries earlier, the French priest Richard Simon, sometimes called the father of Pentateuch criticism for his separation of the Yahwist and Elohist styles, had written:

Si l'Écriture & la Tradition venoient également de Dieu, comme les Juifs prétendent, on devroit sans doute préférer la Tradition, qui explique nettement les Mystères, à un Texte qui est rempli d'obscurités & d'équivoques.

If Scripture and Tradition come equally from God, as the Jews claim, then one must surely prefer Tradition, which explains the Mysteries clearly, to a text which is full of obscurity and equivocation.

And elsewhere:

Les Catholiques, qui sont persuadés que leur Réligion ne dépend pas seulement du Texte de l'Écriture, mais aussi de la Tradition de l'Église, ne sont point scandalisés de voir que le malheur des tems & la négligence des Copistes ayent apporté des changemens aux Livres Sacrés, aussi bien qu'aux Livres profanes. Il n'y a que des Protestans préoccupés ou ignorans qui puissent s'en scandaliser.

The Catholics, who are persuaded that their religion does not depend on the text of Scripture alone but also on the Tradition of the Church, are not at all scandalized to see that the misfortunes of time and the negligence of copyists have brought about alteration in Sacred Books as well as in profane. Only anxious or ignorant Protestants could be scandalized at such a thing.

Simon's words could have been prophetic for Catholicism. They were not. He was silenced. They remain prophetic, however, for Bible criticism today.

In what sense now can it be said that, the Catholic religion having destroyed the Protestant, Catholics will become Protestants? In this sense: Catholic and Protestant Bible scholars alike, having become rationalist historians, will now become Protestants vis-à-vis history. The aspirations of history to comprehensive, harmonious explanation—to a full and final accounting—are exposed for them in redaction criticism in a way that they have not been exposed earlier. This exposure, on the one hand, and that new and general skepticism to which I earlier alluded, on the other, are an invitation to something new, a new appreciation, foreshadowed perhaps in some modern literature. And Jewish Bible scholars, to the extent that they too have become believers in history, will also break with the faith. As (I think) Heine put it, *Wie es sich christelt, so jüdelt es sich*.

The very broadest sweep of Western thought has been from cosmology to epistemology and now, hesitantly, back to cosmology again; or if you will, from the object to the subject and now back to the object. Pre-critical exegesis took the Bible almost as a natural fact. Critical exegesis, preoccupied with religious subjectivity, took it as an historical fact and sought to expose the complex human intent behind it. Post-critical exegesis may take it again as a natural fact, just as post-modern thought takes the human being himself as a natural fact. The language of man, written or spoken, is like his spoor, his scent, his gait, his distinctive laughter—a part of the natural reality of him. It is by remembering this about language, by feeling again the way it felt in the mouth—Yeats said of one of his poems, "I made it of a mouthful of air"—that the great poets of this century are guides to the Bible.

The Bible as we have it is messy. Should we clean up the mess? Cleanliness is next to Godliness, a British and American proverb claims. The Boy Scout promise (one recalls that the Scouts began in England) is: "On my honor I will do my best to do my duty to God and my country, *to be clean*, and to obey the Scout Oath" [emphasis added]. In this spirit, should we clean up the biblical mess?

I do not mean to mock the impulse to cleanliness. All science owes much to it. But the best modern literature reminds us that life is not science and that literature, made of life, cannot ever be as clean as science would have it. The cosmos, it seems to claim, is finally messy. One who believes in a messy cosmos may find a messy Hebrew text oddly cosm-etic. Science is most often a matter of solving the puzzle, but literature, like religious faith, is a matter of being drawn into the game. I take it that this was one of Kierkegaard's objections against Hegel. It may also be the correction that literary sensibility may provide to historicist criticism of the Bible.

At the start of this paper, I asked why the criticism of the modern literatures had had so slight an impact on the study of the Bible. My answer was that the study of the Bible had been, until recently, an historical study and, indeed, an historical study with a particularly lofty sense of its own responsibilities. As their faith in history has become shaky, I said, students of the Bible have been more inclined to take a literary approach to their text, and I then argued for the relevance in Bible studies of an aesthetic of willed confusion like one familiar in much modern literature.

Let me now point out, and even insist, that the aesthetic of modern literature is by no means the aesthetic of modern literary *criticism*. It does not follow, then, that if Bible critics may be assisted toward a fresh understanding of their text by reading Joyce and Pound, they will also be so assisted by reading Bloom and Derrida. No, the aesthetic of literary criticism—in particular, the aesthetic of recent, extremely theoretical literary criticism—is not an aesthetic of willed confusion but one of imperiously willed order. For it, language is not the bodily event we spoke of earlier but, rather, is disembodied writing: not a mouthful of air but a splatter of ink.

No doubt a new generation of Bible scholars, apostate now from historical criticism, could go on to become grammatosophers. As the several generations of historical criticism were concerned *per se* with history, and with the Bible only as a noteworthy historical source, so a new grammatosophical generation could be concerned *per se* with writing and with the Bible only as a noteworthy example of writing. It is salutary to imagine how bracingly concrete, how positively refreshing, after a generation of such discussion a revival of historical criticism would seem. And yet historical and grammatosophical criticism both intend to turn the Bible to some other purpose than its own, or to provide it a purpose if it has none; at all events, not to enjoy it as it is.

The form of Bible study that would take its cue from modern literature rather than from modern criticism is the form urged for all literary study by Roger Shattuck in an article entitled "How to Rescue Literature" (*New York Review*, April 17, 1980, pp. 29–35), namely, a form whose goal and measure is oral performance. Shattuck concedes, as would I, that literature is both speech and writing. At one moment, its scriptural character may require emphasis; at another, its oral character. At the present moment, Shattuck believes, it is the oral character that requires emphasis. I agree, and add that the oral character of the biblical literature both particularly requires this emphasis and can particularly reward it.

Of all the masterworks preserved in the West, none has had the history or, even today, the practice of oral interpretation that the Bible has. We are not accustomed to regard the Jewish and Christian liturgies as works of art; or if in some (perhaps musicological) context they are so regarded, we are not accustomed to allow their artistic character any role in the exegesis of the biblical texts. If, however, oral interpretation, as in the liturgy, were considered relevant for the academic study of the Bible, that study would receive a powerful impetus toward the physical, the vocal, and thence toward an appreciation of the aesthetic effect of the texts in the order in which we have them.

Typically, the meaning of the texts is scarcely adverted to in their liturgical performance, but there is no reason why it might not be, even as the sound of the words releases the aesthetic force of a perhaps willfully confused passage in an infra-conscious, physically inescapable manner. The typical synagogue or church performance is oral but not interpretative; the typical classroom analysis is interpretative but not notably oral. And yet both dimensions are necessary, for what makes language different, as an artistic medium, from pigment or music or gesture is, precisely, that it both sounds and signifies.

Philosophical questions about writing are as endless as philosophical questions about man—and as legitimate in their endlessness. The critical attempt to answer them will not be called off. As for historical scholarship, new critical editions of the Bible in the radical sense earlier indicated may well begin to appear and may even be the crown of the academic tradition that will have produced them. But around these "critical enterprises," as the entrepreneurs like to call them, we may begin to see an accompanying, post-critical love for the physical, accidental, primitive beauty of the thing, this Bible thing, a love for which the model is the *bar mitzvah* boy rehearsing his chant or the acolyte memorizing his responses, a love that leaves the critic no less free to improve the text but slightly more inclined to try simply enjoying it as it is.